Great Ideas in Retailing

Retail Management
A Strategic Approach
11th Edition

Barry Berman
Joel R. Evans

Prentice Hall

Boston Columbus Indianapolis New York San Francisco Upper Saddle River

Amsterdam Cape Town Dubai London Madrid Milan Munich Paris Montreal Toronto

Delhi Mexico City Sao Paulo Sydney Hong Kong Seoul Singapore Taipei Tokyo

Editor-in-Chief: Eric Svendsen
Acquisitions Editor: James Heine
Editorial Project Manager: Kierra Kashickey
Production Project Manager: Ann Pulido
Operations Specialist: Arnold Vila

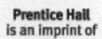

www.pearsonhighered.com

10 9   8   7   6   5   4   3   2   1

ISBN-13: 978-0-13-608799-1
ISBN-10: 0-13-608799-X

PREFACE

Great Ideas in Retailing is specifically designed to accompany *Retail Management: A Strategic Approach,* 11th Edition.

Great Ideas in Retailing is divided into three parts:

- Long Cases—This section consists of 5 cases ranging in length from 5-9 pages. All of these cases are suitable as major class assignments. You may wish to assign them for presentation by teams.

- Short cases—This section is comprised of 29 shorter cases that are generally 2-4 pages in length. These are suitable for shorter assignments or for in-class discussion.

- Chapter-Based Exercises—There is one exercise per chapter (suitable for assignments and for in-class discussion), as well as an integrative case (suitable for a team presentation).

Our goals in developing *Retail Management* and in editing *Great Ideas in Retailing* have been to focus on the exciting and dynamic aspects of retailing (and a course in retailing) and to provide instructors with a large amount of flexibility and background material. We hope that you will comment on this approach.

Barry Berman (mktbxb@hofstra.edu)
Joel R. Evans (mktjre@hofstra.edu)

CASE CONTRIBUTORS

We thank these individuals for contributing cases and exercises to this book:

Irfan Ahmed, Sam Houston State University
Anne Heineman Batory, Wilkes University
Stephen S. Batory, Bloomsburg University
Vicki Budd, College of St. Scholastica
Edward C. Brewer, Murray State University
Doreen Burdalski, Albright College
Howard W. Combs, San Jose State University
Neill Crowley, St. Joseph's University
Phyllis Fein, Westchester Community College
John Fernie, Heriot-Watt University
Suzanne Fernie, Fife College of Further and Higher Education
Jonathan N. Goodrich, Florida International University
Michele M. Granger, Southwest Missouri State University
Terence L. Holmes, Murray State University
Brian R. Hoyt, Ohio University
Gale A. Jaeger, Marywood University
Carol Kaufman-Scarborough, Rutgers University, Camden
Doris H. Kincade, Virginia Tech University
Mark Leipnik, Sam Houston State University
Michael R. Luthy, Bellarmine University
Suzanne G. Marshall, California State University, Long Beach
Sanjay S. Mehta, Sam Houston State University
Allan R. Miller, Towson State University
Michelle Morganosky, University of Illinois at Urbana-Champaign
Sandra Mottner, Western Washington University
John J. Newbold, Sam Houston State University
Denise T. Ogden, Pennsylvania State University, Lehigh Valley
Michael J. Pesch, St. Cloud State University
Carolyn E. Predmore, Manhattan College
Leigh Sparks, University of Stirling
Constance Ulasewicz, San Francisco State University
Valerie L. Vaccaro, Kean University
Ginger Woodard, East Carolina University
Boonghee Yoo, Hofstra University

Barry Berman
Joel R. Evans

HOFSTRA UNIVERSITY

Matrix Linking Long and Short Cases
with *Retail Management: A Strategic Approach*, 11E Text Part Numbers

	Part I	Part II	Part III	Part IV	Part V	Part VI	Part VII	Part VIII
LONG CASES:								
1. Allie's Meat & Grocery	X	X						X
2. Autobytel.com		X	X					
3. Bo Diddley's	X	X	X	X	X			X
4. Coach		X	X			X		X
5. Mystery Shopping	X		X					
SHORT CASES:								
1. B&Q	X							
2. Bari's Department Store						X		
3. Basically Bagels							X	
4. Beverages and More!	X	X						X
5. Burj Al Arab, The	X		X					
6. Calle Ocho							X	
7. Cook 'N Store		X						
8. Cross-Cultural Menu			X					X
9. Custom Ski Pants					X	X		
10. Deep Water Diving						X		
11. Dogwood Kennel		X	X					X
12. Frozen Yogurt Delight		X						
13. Forman Mills			X	X				X
14. Geo. Info. Systems				X				
15. Golden Fleece, The						X		
16. Hayfield House						X		
17. Island Grill	X				X			
18. Just a Joke					X			
19. Large Retail. Demands	X	X				X		
20. Larissa's	X	X						
21. Loan, The			X					
22. Mall Anchors Away		X					X	
23. Prince of Cruises, The				X				
24. Rehab Start	X			X				X
25. Sanchez Property Mgt.				X				
26. Sports Motors	X						X	X
27. Sprucetown					X		X	
28. SweatyBetty	X		X		X			X
29. Value Equation, The	X	X			X			

TABLE OF CONTENTS

LONG CASES

CASE 1

Allie's Meat and Grocery

This case was prepared and written by Professor Brain R. Hoyt, Ohio University. Reprinted by permission.

INTRODUCTION

Allie's Meat and Grocery is a third generation neighborhood grocery store located in a Midwest city with a population of 75,000. The original store was started by the Kim family and attached to a restaurant that the family also owned. While the family once owned and operated five grocery stores, its original store closed just over three years ago due to declining sales. The owners explained that the store closing was the result of the neighborhood switching from residential to a commercial and residential mix. Other key managers and some family members wondered if the closing was due to a Kroger superstore opening in a nearby location. The closing has resurrected deep concerns by the owners, managers, and employees as news of a Wal-Mart opening in town within the next year was just released to the local press.

Allie's Meat and Grocery has 85 full time employees, including 7 family members and 13 part-time employees. The organizational structure is very simple with positions in shelving, cashier, customer service, and management departments. The company owns one refrigerated delivery truck that distributes perishables and grocery items from its warehouse to its four remaining stores. Allie's Mart also owns three delivery vans that are used for catering, as well as for transshipping inventory among its stores.

Allie's Meat and Grocery's newest store is a 35,000-square-foot state-of-the-art facility that has a full bakery, deli, butcher, and catering operation. Products prepared in this store's kitchen are distributed to the other stores for inventory or special orders. This frees up food preparation in Allie's Meat and Grocery's other stores that can now be used for selling space.

Allie's Meat and Grocery is active in community affairs. It is a member of the local chamber of commerce and a charter member of the historic downtown development committee. It sponsors sporting events, health care awareness efforts, annual parades, and festivals. The chain is a past recipient of the chamber of commerce's "Small Business of the Year" award.

Allie's is best known for its meats, deli, ethnic foods, and its new wine and cheese departments. Its organic fruits and vegetables section, always a strong area of differentiation, has recently been upgraded. Allie's growth and success has been steady but slow. Total corporation sales exceed $3 million, but only its newest store exceeds the $1 million mark in sales. These sales numbers put Allie's Meat and Grocery in a bit of a unique category based on the Food Marketing Institute store category system. Allie's Meat and Grocery is not large enough to be designated as a supermarket but most closely fits the definition of an independent grocer with multiple stores larger than a small corner grocer. Its profit margins have outperformed the food industry average profit margins by an average of 0.25 percent.

MARKET ASSESSMENT

Economic Trends
Total grocery sector sales have been estimated as exceeding $1 trillion, with over $830 billion in retail food alone. The traditional supermarket category makes up almost $460 billion of the $1 trillion. Sales at traditional supermarkets have grown at 1.5 percent per year. Thin profit margins have always characterized the retail food sector and recent data indicate profit after tax has dipped below 1 percent to 0.88 percent. The industry's net profit after tax has dropped each of the last 3 years, according to the Food Marketing Institute.

The average expenditure per week while shopping for groceries is $92.50 ($138 for a family of five with $70.90 spent at a consumer's primary store). Shoppers average 2.2 visits to the grocery store per week.

New construction store size is now averaging 34,000 square feet, the first time the average new store size averaged less than 40,000 square feet (according to the FMI Store Development report of 2004).

Competition
The players in the retail grocery sector have remained the same but the growing shift in power is obvious. The two giants (by category) are supercenters (Wal-Mart, Target, Meijer, Kmart, etc.) and the superstore (Kroger, Giant Eagle, Food Lion, etc.). The fastest growing categories are supercenters (with Wal-Mart leading the way) and wholesale clubs (Sam's, Costco, BJ's). While dollar stores currently have a relatively small market share, dollar stores are being watched closely by all grocery retailers as they expand into groceries. Minor players still include independents (grocery operators with less than 11 retail stores), traditional grocery stores, conventional supermarkets, convenience stores, and "corner grocery stores" (less than $1 million in sales).

Technological Trends
According to some retail analysts, the most dynamic technological advances facing the grocery industry involve front-end checkout (primarily scanning equipment and Radio Frequency Identification [RFID] tag technologies). The scanning technology trends focus on self-scanning hardware that offers cost savings for the grocer and convenience for shoppers. RFID technology provides tracking capabilities from manufacturer/processor to the store shelves.

Two important technological trends that are on the horizon are the role of online ordering capabilities and in-home delivery. Among the options available to firms are (1) semi-extended – online ordering by customers with in-store pickup, (2) fully extended – online ordering by customers and delivery at home from a local store's inventory with a company vehicle, (3) de-coupled extended – online ordering by customers and delivery of grocery products from centralized distribution centers using independent shopping firms, and (4) centralized extended – online ordering by customers with products delivered from distribution centers using company vehicles (or subcontractors with company logos on vehicles).

Legal/Regulatory Factors
Important factors in the legal/regulatory forefront involve food safety, nutrition, and labeling requirements. The Food and Drug Administration recently has focused on food freshness, handling, and illness control. Nutritional focus areas include the newly revised food pyramid and

3

dietary guidelines to maintain a healthy lifestyle. Important new labeling requirements include the separate listing of trans fat on all food products.

MARKET CONDITIONS FOR ALLIE'S MEAT AND GROCERY

The upcoming opening of Wal-Mart has everyone in the city projecting who will benefit and who will lose business after it opens. The city now has two Krogers (one is a Kroger superstore with gas pumps), one Meijer, one Target, one Kmart, one Festival Foods, one Aldi's, 36 convenience stores (with gas), six convenience stores without gas, one deli/convenience store with gas, one health food store, one catering/sit down deli, and one meat market/corner grocery. In the past year, the two Big Bear conventional supermarkets closed as did a poultry processor with a retail storefront.

Allie's has been an innovative and relatively aggressive competitor throughout the years as the company grew from a single store/restaurant to the existing four grocery retail outlets (the restaurant is run as a separate entity by a family member). Allie's was the first grocery store to specialize in health food and Asian and Mexican ethnic food selections. It also was the first bakery and deli to offer full catering options (that included serving and cleanup tasks). Each of its stores has ATMs, uses bar code technology to track inventory, has a loyalty program, and uses integrated promotions (including media advertising, coupons, specials, cooperative advertising, and so on).

Before they moved in any direction, the Allie's management team believed it needed a clearer picture of the opportunities and risks associated with Wal-Mart's market presence. The owners contacted a local university and arranged for a retail management class to focus on four different information sources: a review of the existing RIS (retail information system) data, syndicated research, an environmental scan, and a research project. The information gathering activities were directed by this issue definition statement: "What changes should Allie's make to its basic products and services to strengthen its differentiated position as an independent grocer?"

Research Team Focus and Findings

1. RIS Project Team – This team focused on Allie's own information system. The team collected information from Allie's inventory and purchasing records, its loyalty program (including Allie's Savings Card program), and from other internal secondary sources.

    Key Findings
    *   The average Allie's customer's weekly grocery bill has increased steadily over the past five years reaching this year's high of $105. Families of five or more persons (approximately 35 percent of the customer base) averages over $150 in weekly expenditures.

    *   Although average weekly purchases at Allie's have increased on an overall basis, certain product categories have decreased. These product categories (cereal, milk, bread, canned vegetables, and paper products) correspond to those where strong private labels existed at competitive supermarkets and supercenters.

- Allie's customers are not heavy users of coupons (with the exception of the senior population), do not typically stock up on sale items (with the exception of larger family units), or switch brands based on in-store specials. The lone notable exception is the use of frequent shopper programs (tied to loyalty programs and store card tracking programs).

- Sales of low carbohydrate products have increased steadily across all of Allie's customer base.

- Allie's has experienced an increase in home-cooked meal ingredient products, as well as an increase in prepared (ready-to-serve) meals. Ethnic, gourmet, and health food purchases have increased across the entire customer base.

2. Syndicated Research Team – The syndicated research team's objective was to find useful external secondary sources of information that directly related to the grocery sector, its customers, and any factors that directly influenced the food industry. The team focused on syndicated research (data collected by market research companies that is sold to retailer clients) such as the Food Marketing Institute and Nielsen.

Key Findings
- The national average for grocery expenditures is $92.50 per week with a range based on the size of a family ($55–$142 for a family size of 1 to 5 or more).

- Store purchases at the primary store have decreased from 84 percent in 2003 to 82 percent in 2004 to 77 percent in 2005 of total grocery purchases over a three-year period. Shoppers average 2.2 shopping visits per week with 1.7 visits to Allie's primary store. The top three features consumers indicate as important to them when choosing a primary supermarket are (1) high-quality produce, (2) high-quality meats, and (3) a clean/neat store. Other important features include low prices and fast checkout. Additional considerations were money saving specials, convenient store layout, and personal safety outside of the store. Shifts in the rank of these features are evident across gender and age demographics.

- Shoppers report an increase to trip frequency is influenced by speedier checkouts, quick stop areas at the front of store, and friendly/efficient service employees.

- Since September 11, 2001, there has been a national increase in at-home eating trends. Ninety-two percent of households consume at least one home-cooked meal per week and 83 percent consume at least three home-cooked meals per week. There are differences across demographics.

- Age/generation demographics that differ across many food/eating trends include the purchase of health/organic/ethnic food, the importance of self-checkouts, eating out activity, the use of private-label brands, the use of coupons, and the importance of customer service.

- More than half of supermarket shoppers purchase gasoline at supermarket pumps. The importance of niche food offerings (ethnic, gourmet, health, and organic foods) has also increased.

- Forty-six percent of full-time working women shop during the evening hours; this group is more likely to participate in frequent shopper programs.

- A large percent of shoppers now use warehouse clubs and deep discount groceries as a secondary store based on good value and good bargains. Significant sales at these stores are taken from traditional supermarkets.

- More affluent shoppers (the top spenders in all store categories) frequent specialty stores more often, but also use supercenters for bargains. The next socioeconomic category ("living comfortably") shops most store types (supermarket, supercenter, specialty, and value centers/warehouse clubs) on a relatively even basis. The two bottom socioeconomic categories ("getting by" and "poor") primarily shop supercenters and value centers.

3. Environmental Scanning Team – The scanning team searched sources of information (such as market research studies, food trade articles, and trade association reports) outside of the firm. The focus of their search was on technological advances in the grocery and retail sector that might contribute to competitive advantages for Allie's Meat and Grocery.

    Key Findings
    - While scanning equipment has been available in other retail outlets for many years, it is still relatively new to food retail. Usage is up to almost 50 percent in the supermarket sector. Self-scanners usually have a computer display to guide customers through the checkout process. Customers scan or weigh each of their items as the computer keeps track and then each item is placed in a bagging area. The bagging area doubles as a precise scale to verify items and prevent theft. The computer accepts coupons, store loyalty cards, and the standard methods of payment.

    - Most supermarkets have a self-scanning area made up of four to six scanners. The area is supervised by one attendant (instead of four to six attendants) who assists customers through the process, verifies credit card purchases, handles errors, and performs age checks for alcohol and tobacco purchases.

    - In-aisle checkout scanning equipment puts mobility into the self-checkout system as customers scan product bar codes just before they drop the products into their cart. When they arrive at the checkout line, the scanner data is downloaded and payment is made.

    - Supermarket carts with touch screens will guide shoppers directly to products in any aisle, order from the deli without standing in line, and keep a running tally of purchases. Customers can use a home computer to make up their shopping list, log onto the system when arriving to the store, and let the system organize the trip through the aisles. Similar to the in-aisle, a shopper will scan products and then put them in the cart. When the shopping experience is complete, the cart is taken to the checkout line where the card used in the system is scanned into the register. This variation of the in-aisle system is so new that there is not data or information beyond two store trials in Canada. Customer convenience is the primary driver behind this platform innovation.

- Radio Frequency Identification (RFID) applications have distinct advantages over scanning platforms. RFID tags do not require line of sight for accurate reading (this eliminates the multiple swipes of a product over the scanner until it is correctly read). In addition, the wireless technology can read hundreds of RFID tags in a second. Significant savings can be realized throughout the distribution channels, especially at the case and pallet level where tracking speed reduces labor costs.

- Pre-authorized debit cards (ACH cards) provide a convenient option for purchasing groceries and are often tied to loyalty cards. The smart card uses a memory chip technology to store and process information. It can handle electronic payments and is often used for frequent shopper programs and gift cards.

- Smart shelves can read and transmit data through the Internet to store managers and manufacturers, notifying them when product inventory runs low. No physical inventories would be needed and replenishment of products would be based on automatically generated electronic orders.

- Pre-packaging will begin to replace the current practice of packaging perishables in the store. New packaging methods will extend the shelf life of meat, deli, seafood, and produce items. The stricter controls of the packaging environment with manufacturers will better control temperature, food handling, and exposure to bacteria. Smaller kiosks of fresh items will be premium-priced profit centers and supplement the pre-packaged food items.

Advantages and cautions – Many of the documented advantages of adopting the newest technology are based on cost advantages for the retailer. Where the intended advantages for the consumer are based on convenience, the results are more difficult to quantify. Supermarkets have reported positive results on cost reduction, inventory accuracy, theft control, queue improvements (speed through checkout), and customer satisfaction.

Customers have reported mixed results on the impact that the scanning technology has on convenience. Anecdotal comments from interviews indicate that the system is too complicated, requires too many attendant interventions, and rarely saves time. The IHL Consulting group confirmed in one study that time through the self-scan checkout was longer than regular checkout lines. The study also indicated extreme differences of satisfaction levels across age demographics. In-aisle scanning equipment reported results are a bit better than the checkout scanners, but still with some formidable barriers toward high-level customer satisfaction. The access to prices, and a running subtotal is very convenient for shoppers who have used this technology.

RFID technology must be standard throughout the distribution channel to gain a significant advantage. RFID and Smart Shelves address the enormous fears of stock inconsistencies. Running out of stock disappoints customers and reduces revenue. On the contrary, overstocking ties up huge dollar amounts.

4.   Primary Research Team – The research project team was responsible for collecting primary data on various customer satisfaction areas that might provide value added opportunities to combat the cost advantages of supercenters (Wal-Mart) and grocery superstores. The team discussed conducting customer surveys but settled on conducting an extensive mystery shopping project that included each of the four stores owned by Allie's Meat and Grocery, as well as retail food distributors in the area. The team also used mystery shopping at Wal-Mart's closest supercenter store.

Mystery shopping (1) provides a diagnostic tool to identify weak points in basic and value-added service delivery areas, (2) highlights areas of improvement through linking appraisal, training, and reward systems, and (3) assesses the competitiveness of Allie's customer service by benchmarking it against the service offerings of competitive food retailers.

The categories reflected in the mystery shopping effort include: customer contact areas, checkout process accuracy, general satisfaction, service quality gaps, responses by the chain to E-mails, and waiting line effectiveness. Each of these categories was measured by multiple items. Each type of food retailer in Allie's geographic area was sampled including traditional supermarkets, superstores, supercenters, convenience stores, wholesale clubs, dollar stores, and other niche stores (health food store and deli). A minimum of seven separate mystery shopping experiences per store were used to assess a store's performance.

Key Findings
- Customer Contact – This section included greetings initiated by service counter employees at the deli and checkout areas, offers of assistance, service employees' degree of knowledge, and service employees comments thanking customers for patronage. Allie's service performance was ranked highest among all categories (traditional supermarket, superstores, etc.); superstores Wal-Mart and Meijer were next; and then other outlets fell into much lower performance categories. Kroger (a supermarket chain) and a convenience chain ranked the lowest in this category.

- Checkout Process – This section included variables such as checkout time speed, packaging (Were items packed without crushing? Were frozen foods packed with like items? Were raw meats packed separately? Were produce and refrigerated products packed separately?). Allie's Meat and Grocery was ranked highest along with superstores (Wal-Mart and Meijer) and health food stores. Kroger and other supermarkets lagged behind, along with convenience stores.

- Complaint and Service Recovery – This section included immediate involvement in the resolution process by service employee (vs. waiting until a specific manager was present), complaint and recovery process (the next steps if a consumer was still not satisfied), indication of improvement (i.e., cash back for a

8

dented can without recording conditions or explanations), apologies offered, and recovery attempts made above resolution outcome (i.e., cash back for a spoiled product and coupons for a free product). Wal-Mart was ranked highest by a large margin in this service area with supermarkets next and followed by Allie's, convenience stores, and other specialty stores.

- Waiting Line Efficiency – This section studied checkout line capacity (enough lines to handle traffic), whether baggers were equally distributed among lines, checkout flow (price checks, scanning problems, payment transaction delays, self-scan delays), service efficiency in deli/bakery areas, and transaction and bagging lag time (wait time after transaction completed). Allie's ranked in the "middle of the pack" in this area with no real dominant player or store type leading this area.

- Service Gap Analysis – This section of service performance studied gaps between actual experiences and expectations (stated service levels and actual experiences) in promotions versus adequate product inventory or product quality, stated attitudes of employees and actual experience, and stated excellence areas and actual experience. Allie's again ranked highest in this area followed closely by Wal-Mart with a large separation between superstores and convenience stores.

- Physical Environment – This section of service performance includes cleanliness of the parking lot, aisles, and bathrooms, handicap access areas, adequate number of carts that were both clean and dry, special equipment for children and handicapped shoppers, comfortable store temperature, adequacy of aisle width, and adequacy of signage.

Question:

1. Develop a comprehensive plan to improve Allie's competitive position in light of Wal-Mart's arrival. Separate the plan by time period: (a) immediate responses by Allie's, (b) responses at Wal-Mart's opening, and (c) responses within six months of Wal-Mart's opening.

CASE 2

Autobytel.com: Understanding the Customer

This case was prepared and written by Professor Carol Kaufman-Scarborough, Rutgers University School of Business – Camden. Reprinted by permission.

"Every nine seconds an American car shopper requests a vehicle through Autobytel."

INTRODUCTION

Can anything be bought and sold on the Web? This question has been analyzed for over a decade by retail professionals, analysts, and students alike. Not too many years ago, consumers and industry analysts argued that while nondurable products are sold online every day, shoppers would never feel confident to purchase something as costly and important as a used or new car on the Web. The argument was that auto shoppers would not feel secure in searching for and comparing cars by merely looking at photos and reading descriptions. This line of logic further stated that consumers wanted to look at and test drive cars themselves, as well as symbolically "kick the tires."

Today's online auto marketplace has told us that these original perceptions have been largely incorrect. Automobiles can now be compared across models and brands from the convenience of one's home or office, and then purchased through dealer contacts made through an online network. Current online auto sites demonstrate both the use of innovative technology, as well as an excellent understanding of the used and new car purchaser's consumer decision process. This case specifically focuses on the first online auto Web site, Autobytel.com.

Autobytel.com's History
Autobytel is "an Internet automotive marketing services company" that owns and operates several automotive Web sites, including www.myride.com, www.autobytel.com, www.autoweb.com, www.car.com, www.carsmart.com, and www.autosite.com. Autobytel currently only conducts business in the United States, is headquartered in Irvine, California, and employs 225 people.

Autobytel was launched in 1995 as the world's first auto-buying Web site by Peter Ellis, a former auto dealer. It has always operated on a simple premise that links prospective car buyers to dealers through an online lead-generation system. Contact information is provided to dealers in the shopper's local area usually within minutes, but not more than within several hours of the initial online inquiry. Since its founding, millions of car buyers have purchased both used and new autos online, generating billions of dollars in car sales for dealers. Autobytel.com has also been a promotional innovator. In 1996, it was the first Internet company to advertise during the Super Bowl.

As the online auto business evolved, Autobytel's competition has became more complex, ranging from small, local auto dealers to large multi-brand automotive networks. Its competition

10

includes traditional bricks-and-mortar auto dealers, multi-brand auto dealers, auto manufacturers' online sites, and pure online competitors. Shoppers can now search for cars from automotive dealerships such as AutoNation, CarMax, Lithia Motors, Penske Automotive Group, Asbury Automotive Group, and Sonic Automotive. Once shoppers have made decisions about the brand and/or models they are seeking, they can also visit manufacturers' sites directly, such as Honda.com and Toyota.com, or conduct a search for a specific used car on auction sites such as eBay.

In 1998, 1.6 million car buyers submitted purchase requests through Autobytel's Web site. In that year, Autobytel added numerous features to its site including online auctions and auto insurance sales. In 1999, Walden Media, a research company, conducted a nationwide research study in which participants evaluated several facets of online car shopping, including searching for a car, negotiating with dealers, and building relationships with car dealers. The survey found that many consumers were not pleased with some of the features of automotive Web sites. Some consumers also found that many of the sites were difficult to use. Edmunds.com, which listed extensive product information on brands and specific models, placed first among those surveyed, while Autobytel was ranked last. Autobytel and other firms responded by radically redesigning their sites.

In 2001, hundreds of local dealers dropped Autobytel, citing fees that were too costly. During this same time period, auto manufacturers, such as Ford and Toyota, also developed their own Web sites that provided leads to dealers at much lower costs than Autobytel. Autobytel's CEO at that time, Mark Lorimer, felt that Autobytel provided customers with a unique advantage to the manufacurer's Web sites: impartiality. According to Lorimer, a service such as Autobytel can effectively match an uncertain consumer with a large number of dealers representing multiple auto manufacturers with a single Web site visit.

Design and Redesign Challenges

Like many online and offline businesses that sell durable goods, automotive sites need to manage repeated customer visits. Providing unique and fresh information becomes especially important in maintaining a customer's interest in the site over time. In this environment, a Web site needs to be informative, entertaining, and current.

IT analysts argue that a successful and enduring Web site should be analyzed in terms of three simple concepts: usefulness, ease of use, and enjoyment experienced by its users. These concepts underlie the Technology Acceptance Model (TAM) that helps developers better understand whether shoppers will accept and use a new technological design. *Usefulness* centers on how the technology can improve the user's performance. *Ease of use* evaluates various aspects of the process of shopping online, especially whether the Web design allows individuals to shop in the way that they desire. And *enjoyment* measures whether the Web site user has fun using the Web site. One academic researcher suggests that these three concepts can identify whether a Web design and/or redesign will be effective in retaining shopper interest over time.

Applying these concepts to Autobytel, *usefulness* relates to the following dimensions:
- Does the new Web site's design help consumers become more effective in searching for cars?
- Does the new Web site's design help consumers become more effective in evaluating specific cars?

- Does the Web site help consumers find vehicles with the desired features they are seeking (such as diesel engines, 7-person seating capacity, or four-wheel drive)?
- Does the Web site improve a consumer's ability to shop for a car (by virtue of greater selection, lower prices, or obtaining a desired color combination)?
- Are consumers more likely to buy a car when they use one Web site rather than another?

Ease of use can be applied as follows:
- Is the Web site clear and understandable to the typical car shopper?
- How many specific actions are required to secure the required information?
- How much effort is required to compare alternative vehicles?
- Does the Web site allow a consumer to configure a car and see the impact of changing selected features on total cost?
- Is the Web site overly technical?
- Are rebates and other incentives (such as low-cost financing) easily ascertainable?

Determining whether the auto site is *enjoyable* could include the following:
- Is the Web site fun to use?
- Is the Web site exciting?
- Does the site contain information that makes the shopper come back for repeat visits?
- Does the site provide interesting graphics?
- Does the site effectively use video components?
- Do people return to the site even when not shopping for a car?

What Happened

Autobytel's site designers attempted to address some of these issues by adding various features. In 2000, Autobytel took the unusual step of creating a superstore on its site that sold such items as flowers to video games. Other initiatives included promotions specifically targeted at women, who traditionally are unhappy with their treatment in auto salesrooms, and at Hispanic consumers, who prefer communication in Spanish. These strategies did not succeed.

Auto manufacturers' and other direct competitors' Web sites continued to grow in popularity. Autobytel slashed costs in an effort to become profitable; about 15 percent of its workforce was laid off in 2002. Even though it survived the dot-com crash, Autobytel found itself at a crossroads. Autobytel's management concluded that in order to survive, the company needed to radically overhaul its business model. Autobytel acquired several competitors and went through a series of restructurings in 2003 through 2005.

In 2005, Autobytel turned its attention back to better understanding its customers. In addition, the firm carefully reanalyzed its Web site. A major problem that received management's attention involved questionable leads that were sent to dealerships. A questionable lead could contain an incorrect telephone number or a wrong E-mail address, which prevented a dealer from sending vehicle price quotes to a consumer.

Autobytel's New Retail Strategy

Despite various improvements to its Web site, the years that followed did not provide the hoped for recovery for Autobytel (which posted a net loss of $6.3 million in 2005). In March 2006, AOL veteran and former senior vice-president Jim Riesenbach took over as Autobytel's CEO. He immediately developed and implemented a major turnaround plan. Part of this plan involved developing a more thorough understanding of the auto shopper's search process. This included conducting interviews with shoppers to ascertain exactly what information they wanted as part of the online information and shopping process.

Riesenbach viewed Autobytel's mission as "providing the Web's most convenient and comprehensive automotive consumer experience, in turn creating new marketing value—across the purchase and ownership life cycle—for car dealers, automakers, and other automotive marketers." The online process is popular with today's shoppers and should succeed, provided that the Web design meets the needs of everyone in the channel.

Current-Day Site Design Upon logging on to the site, shoppers can now research both new and used cars. Both reviews and price quotes are available for new cars, with research and Kelley Blue Book listings provided for used cars. Auto financing information can also be analyzed.

Autobytel's new vehicle purchasing service enables consumers to shop for and select a new vehicle through its multiple online venues, such as www.autobytel.com, www.autoweb.com, www.car.com, www.carsmart.com, and www.autosite.com. Autobytel also enables shoppers to research such information as auto pricing, features, specifications, and colors.

Autobytel's used car program allows consumers to search for a certified or noncertified used vehicle according to specific search parameters, such as the price, make, model, mileage, year, and location of the vehicle. The used car program locates specific used cars, shows the dealer's location, and displays an actual digital photograph of the vehicles that satisfy the search criteria. Complete vehicle history reports are also available for a minimal fee that list the major repair and accident record for any listed vehicle.

The Dealers Rebuilding the trust of Autobytel's dealer network was also a priority to Riesenbach. Dealers were visited over a several-month period to learn their perceptions, problems, and suggestions. A Dealer Advisory Board was also created. One general problem uncovered was that auto dealers have been critical of the quality of customer leads generated by online auto sites. Some dealers argued that many of the leads did not result in sales since many shoppers were simply browsing and not at the stage of purchasing a car. These critics argued that Autobytel responded too quickly to consumers' initial inquiries, pushing Autobytel to submit a request for leads before consumers were ready to make a purchase commitment. Many auto shoppers required other types of information first, such as financing and leasing information, as well as recommendations from recent car buyers. These insights enabled Autobytel to redesign its online strategy to provide auto shoppers with the information they want and need prior to making a purchase or asking for a price quotation.

Understanding the Customer A recent Autobytel survey revealed that many auto buying consumers wanted less, but more relevant, information prior to determining what car would best meet their specific needs. This survey revealed that information overload can block the shopper from making any decision at all. Information generated by searching by brand, year, or body style are likely to give consumers the control they want to manage the search process and its volume of results.

Another issue centered on female shoppers being particularly uncomfortable or resistant to using the Internet for automotive research and purchasing. This perception can be overcome through creating Web sites that are trustworthy, as well as fun to use.

New Technologies That "Keep in Touch"   A review of competitors' automotive Web sites revealed that many online sites had features including makes, models, and prices levels. To "break away from the pack," Autobytel's multiple Web sites seek to empower automotive consumers with the tools they need to gain information, make contacts, and buy with confidence.

Autobytel's Rapid Response system, introduced in 2007, improved the nature of the relationship between car buyers and auto dealers. The process begins when a potential shopper submits a purchase request on one of Autobytel's websites. The Rapid Response system automatically phones the relevant dealer(s) and provides the dealer with all contact information, as well as a listing of the specific vehicles that most interest the customer. Road Response enables the dealer to place an immediate call to the prospect upon receiving his or her information. Auto dealers that have used this system have stated that this quick contact provides credibility and desired service.

In late 2007, Autobytel took the bold move of launching an innovative, consumer-driven flagship Web site, www.myride.com, that Autobytel described as "the first vertical search experience for the automotive marketplace." This site facilitates user-generated commentary such as video, audio podcasts, photos, blogs, and message boards.

Some measures of the success of www.myride.com include tracking the amount of time that members spend on the site with each visit, how often their visits occur, and what types of features are used. In addition, a measure of consumer involvement might identify the number and types of posts that individuals have made as they connect aspects of their lives with the online community. For instance, while the clear majority of the posts focus on automotive issues, several persons posted photos of themselves, friends, children, and even of birthday celebrations.

CONCLUSION

Financial performance measures indicate that this new approach is working and that Autobytel is on its way to a turnaround in profitability. Autobytel recorded revenues of $84.4 million during its 2007 fiscal year, a decrease of 0.8 percent compared to 2006. The operating loss of the company was $23.2 million during 2007, as compared to an operating loss of $39.8 million in 2006. The net loss was $5.4 million in fiscal 2007, compared to a net loss of $31.5 million in 2006.

Questions:

1.   Identify the strategic issues that led to Autobytel's problems.

2.   Are the changes made by Autobytel likely to be successful? Why or why not?

3.   Assume that you are going to replace the car you (or a friend) drive now.
    a. Pick a make and model, and see how much information you can find for both used and new versions using traditional media (e.g. the newspaper).
    b. Then go to the MyRide.com Web site and another competing Web site of your choice. Try to find the same information from each site.
    c. Compare the results of your two searches, both offline and online.

4. Use the Technology Acceptance Mmodel to evaluate MyRide.com.
   a. Was MyRide useful? Would a buyer be able to make a decision after using the Web site, or would additional information be needed? Was any necessary information missing? Would you be able to come to a decision about a car using the information available on MyRide.com?
   b. How easy was it to use MyRide.com? Did all the elements work as expected?
   c. Is the MyRide.com site fun to use? Would people come back to the site even if they were not going to buy a car?

5. Consider Autobytel's mission as stated by the CEO. How can an online auto retailer create value for all parts of the marketing channel—for car dealers, automakers, and other automotive marketers?

6. What lesson from the Autobytel example can be applied to other online retailers?

7. Honda, together with several other auto manufacturers, maintains sections of its sites where shoppers can "build" their own cars. Visit Honda's Web sites and evaluate your reaction to it in comparison to buying a Honda on Autobytel.com. The "Build and Price Your Honda" page is found at http://automobiles.honda.com/tools/build-price/models.aspx.

CASE 3

Bo Diddley's

This case was prepared and written by Professor Michael J. Pesch, St. Cloud State University, Minnesota; Professor Boonghee Yoo, Hofstra University, New York; and Professor Vicki Budd, College of St. Scholastica, Minnesota. Reprinted by permission.

INTRODUCTION

It was the worst day yet of the cold and blustery Minnesota winter in early 2002. A snowstorm had already dumped 18 inches, and another 6 to 10 inches was expected. "This is great for business," Mary Mountain thought sarcastically as she stopped at yet another red light on Division Street. Making her way from the 25th Avenue restaurant to the Division restaurant, a mere three miles, took her 20 minutes on this particular day.

Mountain certainly did not have a problem finding a parking spot as she pulled into the snow-covered parking lot and climbed out of her car into a two-foot drift. She had just shoveled an hour ago, but the snow was drifted halfway up the front window. She opened the door to the restaurant and felt the warmth on her face, stomped the snow off her feet, and looked up to see John Forsythe, her business partner and brother. Cold and disheartened, Mary said, "John, what are we going to do? Look at this place! The restaurant is empty. Seems we never have enough customers to fill this place to capacity, even on days when we're not getting three-foot snowstorms! And the same thing is true of the two other St. Cloud restaurants."

15

"Mary, we've got to follow the customer demands," said John. "Soup and sandwiches are no longer enough any more. We've got to expand our menu to include burgers and fries, and pizza. You know, the kind of stuff college kids love." Frustrated, Mary said, "But that will only complicate my life even more. I can't seem to keep my arms around these three restaurants the way it is, much less add additional labor-intensive menu items. Besides, Bo Diddley's was founded on the simple concept of healthy, simple, quick food that customers like. We can't lose sight of that."

Company History

Bo Diddley's began as John Forsythe's dream in 1981 when the first Bo Diddley's restaurant opened in St. Joseph, Minnesota, a small town of about 3,000 people, located just outside of St. Cloud. St. Joseph was home to the College of St. Benedict and St. John's University. St. Joseph was a sleepy town that nearly doubled in population during the school year while the students were around. The College of St. Benedict was located just a few blocks from Bo Diddley's. St. John's University, located at the edge of a wooded lake, was about six miles away. Students loved the restaurant, which served soup, sandwiches, soft drinks, and beer. It was a place off campus for them to study, to meet friends, to listen to jazz, blues, or folk music, and to catch a quick bite to eat. The only other restaurants in the entire town were one small pizza shop and a local "family-style" diner.

Students who attended St. John's and St. Ben's were mostly traditional-aged students in their late teens to early twenties, were single, and came from backgrounds with above average to significantly above average household incomes. The vast majority of students were full-time and graduated within four years with a bachelor's degree. The cost of tuition, books, room, and board for one year is approximately $25,000.

John Forsythe's success with his college town restaurant led him to imagine an expansion into St. Cloud, just seven miles east of St. Joseph, where he could implement the same strategy to sell Bo Diddley's to the 15,000 students who attended St. Cloud State University (SCSU). SCSU was the second-largest public university in Minnesota. The student population was economically and demographically diverse in terms of age, household income, marital status, and student status (part-time or full-time). About half of the students graduated in four years or less with a bachelor's degree. The cost of tuition, books, room, and board for one year was approximately $8,500.

In addition to the market opportunity at St. Cloud State, the St. Cloud metropolitan area, with a population of 105,000, was one of the fastest growing regional centers in Minnesota. Starting in the late 1980s and continuing through the current period, St. Cloud attracted significant investment from a wide variety of industries, including retail, health care, banking, restaurant chains, and professional services (legal, accounting, etc.).

In the mid-1990s, John decided to invite his sister, Mary, to join the venture to expand into St. Cloud. Mary agreed to manage the day-to-day operations while John focused more on the strategic side of the business. Although the St. Cloud venture was to be a brother-sister partnership, John would continue to be the sole owner and manager of the St. Joe restaurant.

In February 1997, John and Mary opened the 25th Avenue restaurant. Located two miles west of the SCSU campus, the 25th Avenue site was not exactly a "prime location" to reach SCSU students. Still, it seemed to have good potential. The new restaurant was located between the city's two main traffic arteries and behind a major shopping center. John reasoned that once Bo Diddley's customers from St. Cloud learned about the new location, the restaurant would thrive.

John was right. The 25th Avenue restaurant was so successful that they decided to open another restaurant on Northway Drive in June 1998, about two miles from the 25th Avenue restaurant. The new site was located directly across the street from a large office park for several medical and dental clinics, a YMCA, and the St. Cloud Technical College. Unfortunately, many customers from the 25th Avenue restaurant shifted their business to the Northway restaurant, causing a 35 percent drop in sales at the 25th Avenue restaurant.

The two new restaurants were still a considerable distance from SCSU, John and Mary's original target market. They continued to explore options closer to SCSU, but it took them two years just to find a suitable location. In January 2001, they opened the Division Street restaurant. The Division site was located five blocks north of the SCSU campus and two blocks south of the bustling downtown area. "Finally we'll reach the SCSU students we've been hoping to attract," said Mary. But to their surprise, the clientele was mostly business professionals stopping in for a quick, nutritious bite to eat. Only a small portion of the customer base was students. An additional surprise came when they discovered that immediately after the Division restaurant opened, sales at the 25th Avenue restaurant dropped another 40 percent. See Table 1 for a summary of the four restaurants' characteristics.

Table 1
Restaurant Profiles

Restaurant		St. Joseph	25th Avenue	Northway Drive	Division Street
Year Opened		1981	1997	1998	2001
Owners		John Forsythe	John Forsythe, Mary Mountain	John Forsythe, Mary Mountain	John Forsythe, Mary Mountain
Major neighboring sites		College of St. Benedict; St. John's University; Retail businesses	Retail businesses; Some residential	Medical centers; St. Cloud Technical College; YMCA; Whitney Park	Corporate businesses; St. Cloud State University
Street traffic		Less heavy	Heavy	Heavy	Very heavy
Restaurant visibility		Good	Poor	Excellent	Excellent
Customers	Lunch	Professionals 5%; Blue collar 15%; Students 80%	Professionals 50%; Blue collar 50%; Students 0%	Professionals 80%; Blue collar 15%; Students 5%	Professionals 70%; Blue collar 5%; Students 25%
	Dinner	Families 20%; Students 80%	Professionals 50%; Students 50%	Professionals 50%; Students 50%	Professionals 50%; Students 50%

Smoke-free	No	Yes	Yes	Yes
Pub	Yes	No	Yes	Yes
Neighboring competition	Subway; Taco John's	Mexican Village; Leeann Chin	Chinese Buffet; Tom Thumb; Deli	Chinese Buffet; Perkin's
Neighboring complementary retail businesses	A bank; A gas station	Byerly's grocery; Tom Thumb gas	Tom Thumb gas	Coborn's grocery; Video Update; Kinko's
Distance from the campus of St. Cloud State University	7 miles (West of the campus)	2 miles (West of the campus)	2.5 miles (Northwest of the campus)	5 blocks (Northwest of the campus)
Monthly sales, January 2002	Not available	$9,000	$17,000	$22,000

Despite these disappointments, Bo Diddley's was developing a reputation in the community for being a tasty and health-conscious restaurant. It won Health Partner's (a local HMO) "Healthy Heart Award" for the most nutritious recipes in local restaurants, and the *St. Cloud Times* newspaper's Reader Survey Awards for the "Best Sandwich," "Best Soup," and "Best Quick Lunch."

Catering
In 2001, Bo Diddley's made $1,000 per month at both the Northway and the Division restaurants from catering services. The catering service fit three types of customers: professionals who were too busy to come out for lunch, customers with regular meetings (such as a church board meeting and the Chamber of Commerce), and customers who had special events (such as a school picnic or a graduation party). Customers who used the service easily became repeat buyers because of the good price and food quality. Prices were discounted by 10 percent for sandwiches and an additional 10 percent for $100 or greater in purchases. Catering customers were very complimentary, which made Mary think there was some potential in the catering market.

Promotional Activities
In 2001, Bo Diddley's only advertising activity was a billboard that stood on Division Street between the 25th and Division restaurants. The message on the billboard was clear and simple: "Bo Diddley's—Best Sandwich, Best Soup, and Best Quick Lunch." The letters were in yellow on the black background. Mary paid $200 a month for the billboard, but she was not sure of its effect on the business. She did not advertise in the Yellow Pages because of the expense. For example, the monthly rate for a 3-by-4 inch in-column ad was $300. But she began to believe that the Yellow Pages could be effective in attracting customers who liked Bo Diddley's type of food.

Bo Diddley's coupons appeared almost daily in the *St. Cloud Times* newspaper, whose weekday circulation was 28,000 and on Sunday, 38,000. The *Times* charged nothing for the coupons. A typical coupon read "50% off any sandwich with purchase of sandwich of equal or greater value." The addresses and telephone numbers of the four restaurants were provided on every coupon. The coupons also appeared in the *Chronicle*, the SCSU students' biweekly newspaper, and *Shoppers' News*, a weekly coupon and advertising magazine. About ten coupons were redeemed every day in each restaurant. The major users of the coupons were professionals who had lunch with co-workers, and senior citizens who enjoyed eating out with their spouses or friends. Mary wondered, "I expected that students, given their tight budgets, would like the coupons the most, but they seldom use coupons. I don't understand."

Mary often sponsored SCSU students' sports programs and special campus events. However, a 2001 market survey surprised her because few SCSU students were aware of Bo Diddley's name and what Bo Diddley's was. Most students had no association with Bo Diddley's at all. Mary was frustrated. "This is totally a one-way love relationship. I sponsored their events by giving prizes and donations, but I see no impact on my sales. I don't know how to get my message across to students that this is a great place to eat."

While Mary expressed dismay at the lack of college student customers, many students did patronize the Division Street Bo Diddley's (see Table 1). An unscientific interview sample was conducted on six male college students who were eating lunch together one day at the Division restaurant. Table 2 reports their responses, as well as Mary's responses, to the question, "Why do people eat at Bo Diddley's?"

Table 2
Responses to the Question, "Why Do People Eat at Bo Diddley's?"

From Interview with Six Male College Students
- Good portions
- Fresh ingredients ("The food is great, man.")
- Convenience (Two of the six students "come here every day, man.")
- Good price versus McDonald's "Super-Size" meal

From Interview with Mary Mountain, Co-Owner
"People come because of the quality of our food. We buy the best ingredients: breads, meats, cheese…even the mayonnaise is more expensive than we could get elsewhere, but the taste is superior. The other thing people like is they can get their food within a few minutes after placing their order. The lunch customers really like that. The menu lends itself to quick turnaround times on customer orders: soups, subs, pita sandwiches, cookies, and baklava. Our slogan is 'We offer quality food quick.' "

The 25th Avenue Dilemma
To sort out the situation of the 25th Avenue restaurant, John rummaged through his briefcase and pulled out financial information showing that overall food and beverage costs made up 36.5 percent of total sales and labor costs averaged $5.50 per hour. A sales analysis of all three restaurants revealed that 60 percent of each day's sales were made during the 11:30 to 1:30 lunch hour, 30 percent of sales were made during the 5:00 to 7:00 p.m. dinner hour, and the remaining 10 percent of sales occurred during the non-mealtime hours. Mary retrieved the current employee work schedule at the 25th Avenue restaurant (Table 3).

"What are we going to do, Mary?" John asked. "We just can't continue with all these empty seats. I overheard a customer at the 25th restaurant the other day saying to her friend how much she loved eating there because it's so quiet. Well that's nice, but it's quiet because we're not filling chairs with customers. I say we've got to get more aggressive in going after customers who like cheeseburgers and fries for lunch—traditional American food! And what about pizza? We don't have to drop our sandwiches and soup, just offer more variety to appeal to more customers!"

Mary replied, "I agree, we have to do something. I never thought we would cannibalize customers from the 25th Avenue restaurant as much as we did when we opened Northway and Division, but it's happened. Just look at this sales trend! (Table 4 shows monthly sales in 1997, 1998 and 2001 of the 24th Avenue restaurant. These dates correspond with the initial opening of the 25th Avenue restaurant and with the opening of the Northway Drive and Division Street restaurants). Besides, I don't see the point of running around to three restaurants all day if we

Table 3
The 25th Avenue Restaurant's Daily Labor Schedule by Hours of Operations

Employee	10:00 to 11:00 a.m.	11:00 to 12:00 a.m.	12:00 to 1:00 p.m.	1:00 to 2:00 p.m.	2:00 to 3:00 p.m.	3:00 to 4:00 p.m.	4:00 to 5:00 p.m.	5:00 to 6:00 p.m.	6:00 to 7:00 p.m.	7:00 to 8:00 p.m.	8:00 to 9:00 p.m.	9:00 to 10:00 p.m.
Mic	x	x	x	x	x	x						
Jacki	x	x	x	x	x	x						
Ben		x	x	x								
Kim							x	x	x	x	x	x
Chris							x	x	x	x	x	x

could have almost as many customers with two restaurants. Maybe we should just take our medicine and close the 25th restaurant."

John shook his head. "This sales dip is only temporary. If we add items to the menu and get a marketing plan together, I think we can turn this around. The other thing that I think is holding us back is this crazy no smoking policy. I mean practically every restaurant except ours has a smoking section. Personally, I don't like smoking, but we have to cater to a broader group of customers or we're dead in the water. A smoking section will attract more customers."

Mary sighed and gazed at the ceiling, then said, "This is too much...What are we doing? People come to our restaurant because we're *not* like every other restaurant. Besides, in addition to fryers, grills, and ovens, we'll also have to install a $6,000 air exchange system into each restaurant if we get into burgers, fries, and gyros. Not to mention, more training requirements and probably slower service to customers..."

Mary and John sat looking at each other, wondering what to do.

Table 4
Monthly Sales for the 25th Avenue Restaurant

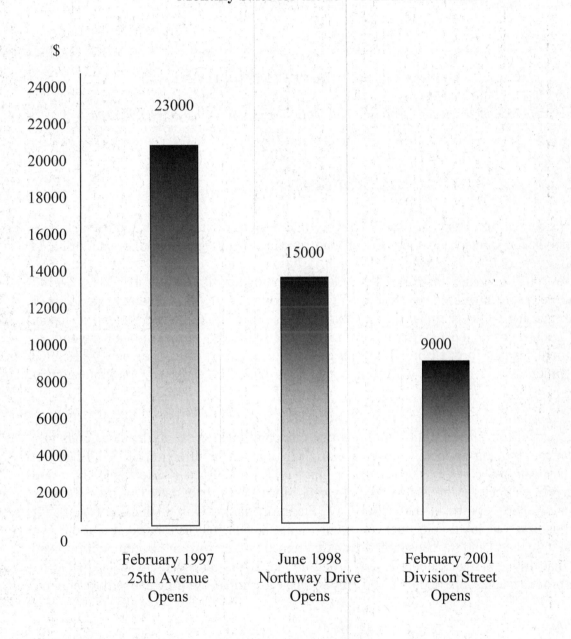

Questions:

1.   What is Bo Diddley's business strategy? What is its distinctive competence?

2.   What is/are the root problem(s) faced by John and Mary?

3.   Should the 25th Avenue restaurant be closed? Explain your answer.

4. What should Mary and John do to address the excess capacity (empty seats) in their restaurants?

5. What are the pros and cons of expanding the menu?

CASE 4

Coach: Expanding an Innovative, Luxury Brand

This case was prepared and written by Professor Valerie L. Vaccaro, Kean University. Reprinted by permission.

INTRODUCTION

Coach, Inc. is a U.S. firm based in New York City that designs, manufactures, and sells luxury accessory goods for women and men. Coach had revenues in 2008 of approximately $3,180 million and over 12,000 employees (of which 3,700 are full-time employees). In 2008, compared to 2007, revenues increased by 21.8%, operating profit rose by 15.5% to $1.147 million, and net profit increased by 18% to $783.1 million. While its products are sold in 21 countries around the world, the majority of Coach's sales occur in the United States and Japan. Recently, Coach repositioned its offerings from conservative-styled American leather goods to become a more fashion-forward brand. Coach now offers a steady stream of newly-designed innovative products and offers a wide range of prices aimed at satisfying multiple market segments.

Coach's successful transition from a family-owned company making sturdy leather goods to a billion-dollar trendy luxury goods firm was accomplished under the direction of Lew Frankfort (Coach's chairman and chief executive officer since 1979) and Reed Krakoff, president and executive creative director (who has worked at Coach since 1996). In a statement from Coach's 2007 Annual Report, Chairman and CEO Lew Frankfort said: "Our distinctive brand, our leadership position, our loyal consumer base, our multi-channel international distribution, and our focus on innovation and the consumer never vary and set us apart from the competition. And the engine that drives these elements is our strong and seasoned management team, fueled by compelling products and supported by an adaptive, dynamic, global sourcing and supply chain."

Competition

In the United States, Coach is the leading premium brand in the luxury leather-goods market, with a market share of over 25 percent in 2007 (up from 17% in 2000), followed by Louis Vuitton at 12 percent, Dooney & Bourke at 7 percent, and 6 percent each for Gucci and Prada.

Japan represents about 40 percent of the global luxury goods market. Coach's market share in Japan increased from 2 percent in 2000 to 12 percent in 2008, making it the number two brand. In 2000, market leader Louis Vuitton had a 33 percent market share, which decreased to 27 percent in 2008; and both Gucci and Prada originally had over 10 percent market share each, but each dropped to less than 10 percent in 2008.

Other competitors in the global luxury goods market include Christian Dior, Fendi, Kate Spade, Juicy Couture, Couture Couture, Armani Exchange, Furla, Tod's, Salvatore Ferragamo, Tiffany, and Versace.

Coach's History

In 1941, Miles and Lillian Cahn began making a limited line of high quality, handmade leather goods in their family-run workshop, which was originally called NY Wallets and Belts. In 1962, NY Wallets and Belts changed its name to Coach and began specializing in fine handbags. Coach opened its first retail store in 1981. In 1985, Coach was acquired by Sara Lee, a large public corporation that expanded Coach's operations by entering foreign markets (such as the UK and Japan (in 1988) and adding factory outlets. In 1998, Coach introduced its first mixed-materials bag, fabric with leather trim that was both cost efficient and popular. In 1999, Coach introduced black nylon bags, began licensing its name to watches, footwear, and furniture, and launched its Web site, www.coach.com.

In 2001, Sara Lee sold back its ownership to Coach, making it an independent company again. Also in 2001, Coach formed a joint venture with Sumitomo, Coach Japan. Four years later, Coach repurchased Sumitomo's 50 percent stake for $300 million, making Coach's Japanese division a 100 percent-owned subsidiary of Coach.

In 2006, Coach entered into an exclusive agreement with BeautyBank, a division of The Estée Lauder Companies, to create fragrances and related beauty products to be sold in Coach's U.S. retail stores. A new global flagship store was opened in Hong Kong in 2008. Coach also announced its plans to enter the Russian market through an arrangement with Jamilco, a distributor with strong experience in marketing luxury brands in Russia.

Key Issues

From 2000 (the year the firm went public) to 2007, Coach had high double-digit increases in profit and sales every year. From June 2002 to June 2007, Coach's average net income growth was an astounding 51 percent per year. In 2008, it was predicted that Coach's net income growth would slow to 11 percent as a result of the recession.

Even with the economic slowdown, Coach planned to continue with its strategy of new product innovation, store expansion, and distribution in the United States, Japan, and China. The key issue according to market analysts is whether Coach can maintain high levels of growth that it has experienced before the worldwide economic downturn. The following summarizes the key strategic challenges that Coach faced in 2008. These include financial issues, brand/positioning and pricing issues, competition, and counterfeit goods.

Financial issues:

- Lower financial performance: slower rate of growth for revenues and income due to slowdown in the U.S. economy. About 75 percent of Coach's total revenues are from the United States.

- Coach stopped reporting revenues from its specialty stores and factory outlets as separate items, reducing transparency. Stock analysts and investors viewed this as a means of masking slower sales at Coach's regular stores with faster growth at its factory. Some analysts argue that too high a proportion of outlet sales might harm Coach's luxury brand.

- From April 2007 to April 2008, Coach's stock decreased more than 40 percent from a record high of $54 per share down to $31.70 per share.

Brand/positioning and pricing issues:

- Coach never discounts at its full-price stores and does not mention its outlet stores on the Web site. Coach originally sold only discontinued merchandise at the outlet stores, but since 2003, it has designed less trendy products for the 40 plus target audience of females who shop its factory outlets. Since December 2007, when sales at full-price stores declined by 1.1 percent, compared to a 20.8 percent increase in December 2006, Coach has begun to offer deeper discounts at its factory outlets.

- Brand image issues: Coach risks having its outlet shops cannibalize a portion of sales from its full-price specialty stores. This may undermine the high-quality image of the brand (making it less exclusive).

Competition:

- There is strong competition in the United States and Japan.

Counterfeit goods:

- Counterfeit luxury fashion accessories such as watches, shoes, and handbags negatively affect sales of branded luxury goods. Brands such as Tiffany, Coach, Louis Vuitton, Cartier, and Burberry are commonly sold as "knock-offs."

Target Markets

According to Bain & Company, a major consulting firm, the $254 billion global luxury goods market consists of three consumer segments: (1) the super rich "absolute" group of consumers who purchase the most expensive brands in the world (e.g., Harry Winston), (2) the "aspirational" luxury middle level market segment of wealthy consumers (who purchase expensive designer brands such as Louis Vuitton), and (3) the "accessible" luxury market segment (consumers with household income between $75,000 and $149,000) who patronize brands such as Coach and Tiffany.

A major problem for Coach and other firms selling accessible goods is that that during the 2007-2008 economic recession, the "accessible" luxury market group heavily cut back on spending. Some industry analysts predict that some "accessible" luxury brand companies may start targeting the super-rich "absolute" luxury market.

In the United States, Coach targets two types of consumers, both of whom are brand loyal. One group include "urban fashionistas"—elite consumers with high income, an average age of 35, college-educated, single or newly married, with a sophisticated city lifestyle, who spend an average of $1,100 per year at Coach's full-price stores (especially in metropolitan locations such as Manhattan, Los Angeles, etc.). Coach's other target market is more of an "aspirational consumer"—"professional moms who want beautiful, well-made brands at low prices" rather than the latest trendy style. These consumers shop at the local mall (in places such as Queens, Staten Island, and towns in New Jersey) or at the outlet stores, and represent between 30 percent and 50 percent of U.S. buyers of Coach products. These aspirational consumers include many first time users and college graduates (many of whom are teachers, social workers, and suburban moms—who spend about $770 a year on Coach products and are, on average, 45 years old and married).

In the United States, in addition to women, about 10 percent of Coach's sales are from men's accessories (e.g., attachés, belts, ties, messenger bags, shoes, hats, etc.). Coach has also recently added small, inexpensive items such as leather wristlets, key chains, and iPod cases to appeal to younger male and female customers.

In China, Coach's primary target market focus is similar to the "aspirational" American consumer. *[Note: Coach's use of the term "aspirational" is actually the equivalent of the Bain & Company's industry term for the "Accessible" luxury market.]* CEO Frankfort describes the market in China as "the emerging middle class who have gone to university and are now getting 30 percent to 40 percent [pay] increases a year as engineers, doctors, bankers, and lawyers. These women are trading up…and are looking for ways to broaden their life, and Coach is one way." Coach also plans to sell to very wealthy luxury consumers in China (who have large purchasing power), but that is not its main target market.

In Japan, Coach's target market consists of women under 35 years old who are looking for a less expensive luxury brand than ones from Europe. Coach's market research found that young Japanese women would rather pay 60,000 yen (approximately $578) for a Coach handbag, and then spend the other 60,000 yen (saved from not purchasing a European luxury handbag) on such goods and services as iPods, day spas, and vacations. This younger target market is different than their mothers, who still buy the more expensive European brands for status symbols such as Louis Vutton, Gucci, and Prada.

Products, Branding, Positioning, and Pricing

In 2000 in the United States, the average female luxury goods consumer bought two handbags. By 2007, that number had doubled to an average of four handbags per year. According to Coach's CEO, Lew Frankfort, the typical Coach customer owns eight Coach handbags. In addition, one finding of market research interviews with thousands of Coach's consumers was that its core customers visit a full-price store about once a month. In response to these store visits, Coach has introduced new styles of products on a monthly schedule, to give consumers a fresh and adventurous shopping experience.

Coach's products include handbags, women's and men's accessories (belts, gloves, scarves, and hats), business cases, wallets, cosmetics cases, travel bags (duffel bags, suitcases, and garment bags), baby accessory products (diaper bags, teddy bears, and picture frames), footwear (women's and men's), outerwear (e.g., fur-trimmed ski parkas), skis, eyewear (sunglasses), watches, jewelry (bracelets, necklaces, charms, and earrings), key chains, iPod cases, and fragrances. In 2007, Coach's three new lifestyle platforms (Signature Stripe, Legacy, and Ergo) were well received by existing customers, and also attracted new customers. The Fall 2008 collection introduced in Coach's full-priced stores included new, more refined, sophisticated, drapey-shaped handbags, made of lighter-weight leather, with patent, glazed, and metallic finishes. Some of the handbags have a new "C" logo pattern that is more subtle than the original more prominent designer logo.

Coach's average-priced handbag used to be about $300 in the United States. In order to reach the less wealthy U.S. consumer, Coach has been introducing purses at lower prices (some around $200). In contrast, in the United States and in Japan, Coach has also started to offer more upscale merchandise as part of the new Legacy line. The Legacy line includes 20 handbags, 20 small leather goods items, 10 footwear styles, and 2 jackets. In Japan, Coach has products with higher price tags for about $1450 (173,250 yen), in addition to Coach handbags that sell for about $500.

Coach's full-price stores never offer discounts or markdowns; prices remain the same at these stores year round. Instead of reducing prices at these full-price stores, older merchandise is moved to Coach's factory outlet locations. Outlet stores also carry less trendy products at lower prices (about 25 percent less than the full price stores).

Outsourcing Manufacturing

Coach has a low-cost competitive advantage with its outsourcing. According to CEO Frankfort, "We make our product in lower-cost countries. Even though the raw materials come from the finest mills and tanneries in the world, we save incredible amounts of money on labor. The average cost in France and Italy is $50 an hour, and a bag could take five hours to produce. Our labor costs are 10 percent of that."

Coach has its products produced by independent manufacturers in the United States, China, India, Hungary, Indonesia, Italy, Korea, Mauritius, Singapore, Spain, Taiwan, and Turkey. Each manufacturer provides 13 percent or less of Coach's total productions. This oursourcing strategy reduces Coach's required assets for manufacturing, lowers labor costs, and reduces reliance on output from one country and one manufacturer.

Multi-Channel Distribution

Coach uses a multi-channel retail network, comprising its own retail stores (full-price and outlets), catalogs, and Web sites (including www.coach.com). Coach's catalogs help stimulate brand awareness and increase sales in stores and on its Web site; and its Web site also helps stimulate in-store sales. In 2006, CEO Frankfort estimated that more than 50 million unique consumers visited Coach's Web site, and about 45 million consumers would visit Coach's stores.

In the United States, the average size store is 2,500 square feet (with about 85 percent of its stores in premium sections of malls and the other 15 percent in shopping district locations). The flagship stores are usually larger. Coach's flagship Manhattan store, located on 57th Street, was expanded to 10,000 square feet; the Beverly Hills store is 3,365 square feet. The company's outlet stores (which carry older, less trendy, less expensive merchandise) are deliberately located at least an hour's drive (about 60 miles) from any of the full-price Coach stores. Coach's indirect channel includes U.S. wholesale and international wholesale distributors that sell its products to upscale stores, including top-of-the-line department stores, to support the luxury brand image. Select international distributors market Coach's products to department stores, freestanding retail locations, and specialty retailers in 21 countries. Coach's current network of international distributors sells to markets such as the United States (primarily Hawaii and Guam), the

Caribbean, Mexico, Korea, China, Taiwan, Hong Kong, Japan, Singapore, Thailand, Malaysia, Australia, New Zealand, Indonesia, Saudi Arabia, the United Arab Emirates, and France.

Table 1 provides an overview of Coach's current distribution and expansion plans. Coach plans to add about 200 more full-price stores in the United States, which would bring its total number of stores (both full-price and outlets) to about 500. Coach also recently bought out its distributor in China and plans to open 50 additional stores there. Coach expects that China will eventually become a larger market than Japan.

Table 1
Coach Distribution: Store and Internet Expansion Plans

Country	Current Distribution	Additional New Distribution Planned Between 2008 and 2013
United States (full-price)	259 stores + Internet + catalog	200 new stores
United States (outlets)	93 factory outlet stores	105 new stores
United States (shop-in-shop in department stores: Macys, Saks, Bloomingdales, Dillard's, Nordstrom, Lord & Taylor)	900 department stores (which make up only 12% of worldwide sales)	N.A. (not available)
Canada	5 stores	20 stores
Japan	118 stores (includes flagship, full-price and some outlets) + Internet + catalog	62 new stores
Japan (shop-in-shop in major department stores)	129 department stores	19 new Internet locations
China	42 stores (19 in Taiwan, 12 in Hong Kong, 11 on the mainland in Shanghai, Beijing, Hangzhou, Shenzhen, and Xi'an)	20 to 50 new stores
Russia	2 stores	15 stores
Greater China, Southeast Asia, and the Middle East	N.A.	30 new Internet locations via distributors
Other countries	Products are also sold in 21 countries via international distributors.	

Marketing Communications

Coach's Web site, www.coach.com, and its catalogs help promote the brand. In addition, Coach runs print advertisements in major fashion and beauty magazines, such as *Vogue* and *InStyle*. The company has run comprehensive Internet campaigns, and regularly E-mails its data base of 10 million customers. When Coach introduced its new fragrance, it distributed 500,000 deluxe miniature samples to its top customers. An additional 1.5 million fragrance vials were placed in magazines and in the firm's catalogs.

Currently, it appears that the firm does not advertise on radio or television, or on outdoor billboards. Coach's advertising campaigns in the United States have not included celebrities, and the firm does not pursue product placement or publicity related to celebrity adoption of the products.

In addition, Coach's store design has played an important role in communicating Coach's upscale image. Coach's Manhattan and Bevery Hills flagship stores have upscale, elaborate exterior designs. Store interiors are decorated with luxurious materials including marble from Carrera, Italy, and walnut or other special woods.

Strong Financial Performance

In 2007, *Business Week's* "Top 50 Best Performers" list included Coach as number two (after the number one-ranked Google). The total U.S. handbag market in 2007 was approximately $6 billion, and Coach had about 30 percent of that market share. Table 2 shows that Coach's revenues increased from 2006 to 2007 by 28.4 percent to $2.6 billion. However, this revenue growth was not as impressive as in previous years. In 2004, Coach's sales revenues increased by 39 percent, and net profit had increased by 79 percent. And in 2005, sales rose by 30 percent and profits by 49 percent.

Table 2
Coach 2007 Financial Data
Direct Versus Indirect Distribution by Geographic Region

Fiscal Year 2007	Amount	Increase from 2006 to 2007
Total sales revenues	$2,612 million ($2.6 billion)	28.4%
Direct to consumer sales (Coach stores in U.S., Japan, etc.)	$2,100 million ($2.1 billion) Includes Internet sales $82 million (80.5% of total revenues)	30% 51% increase in Internet sales
Indirect sales (department stores in U.S., Japan, etc.)	$ 511 million (19.5% of total revenues)	20%
Operating profit	$ 993.4 million	39%
Net profit	$ 663.7 million	34%
Geographic revenues - U.S. 76.4%	$1,996.1 million	33.3%
Geographic revenues - Japan 18.9%	$ 492.7 million	17.2%
Geographic revenues - Other regions 4.7%	$123.6 million	5.9%

Table 3 shows the market share percentage for the global luxury goods market by geographic region. The composition of the market is very different than Coach's revenue sources by country/region. While the U.S. market accounted for 76.4 percent of Coach's total revenues (see Table 2), revenues for LVMH Moet Hennessy Louis Vuitton (LVMH) are more geographically diversified. Twenty-six percent of LVMH's revenues come from the United States, 37 percent from Europe, 30 percent from Asia, and 7 percent from other markets.

Table 3
Global Apparel, Accessories, and Luxury Goods Market Share—2007 Data

Country	Market Share
Asia-Pacific	34.1%
Europe	30.7%
United States	20.6%
Other	14.6%

An analysis of Coach's sales by product line (see Table 4) shows that handbags make up 67 percent of its total sales, women's accessories account for 23 percent, footwear and watches are 4 percent of sales, and men's accessories, outerwear (gloves, hats), and business cases and suitcases are each 2 percent of sales. Other products that Coach sells, such as jewelry and fragrances, were not included in this company analysis.

Table 4
Coach Percentage of Sales by Product Line

Coach product lines	Percentage of Sales
Handbags	67
Women's accessories	23
Footwear and watches	4
Men's accessories	2
Outerwear (gloves, hats)	2
Business cases and suitcases	2

Table 5 provides product category sales data for global luxury goods. Leather goods, jewelry, and watches, categories stressed by Coach, account for 18.1 percent of this market.

Table 5
Global Luxury Goods–Product Category Share in 2007

Product Category	Percentage Share
Womenswear (apparel)	47.5
Menswear (apparel)	31.9
Jewelry	12.0
Leather Goods	4.4
Infantswear (apparel)	2.6
Watches	1.7

CONCLUSION

Since 2000, when Coach became a public corporation, it has successfully transformed itself into a trendy luxury goods designer, manufacturer, and retailer, with fast-paced new product innovation. From 2000 to 2008, Coach experienced double-digit growth in revenues and profits, but starting in 2007, the rate of growth has slowed, and the firm's stock price has significantly declined.

While Coach has plans for continued expansion in the United States and Japan, as well as new store openings in China and Russia, some industry analysts are concerned that Coach may be missing out on key opportunities for growth. They are further worried that high demand for the firm's outlet shops could erode Coach's brand equity.

Questions

1. What new product opportunities could Coach pursue?

2. What other countries or regions of the world should Coach consider expanding into and why?

3. How could macro-environmental industry trends (e.g., demographic population trends, green marketing trends, etc.) affect Coach?

4. What other kinds of marketing communications could Coach do that it does not currently include in its promotion mix?

5. Based upon the economic climate, should Coach follow more of a downmarket strategy? What are the pros and cons of a downmarket focus?

6. Should Coach start offering discounts or markdowns at its specialty stores? Identify the advantages and disadvantages of this strategy.

6. What strategies could Coach employ at its Web site (www.coach.com) and in its stores to enhance customer relationship management?

CASE 5

Mystery Shopping Grocery Stores: Finding Opportunities to Build Customer Loyalty

This case was prepared and written by Professor Brian R. Hoyt, Ohio University. Reprinted by permission.

Large retail grocers such as Kroger, Safeway, and Wal-Mart, as well as specialty retail grocers such as Whole Foods are all maneuvering to maintain growth and profit margins in the midst of a sluggish economy and higher food prices. During the current recession, food prices have skyrocketed with monthly increases higher than at any time in the past 20 years. While some large retailers have been able to raise prices along with inflation without constraining unit sales volume, others have less flexibility in raising prices. With the $535 million grocery industry in the midst of a major recession, the major grocers such as Wal-Mart (with a 15 percent market share), Kroger (with a 10 percent market share), and Safeway/Costco/SuperValu/Sam's Club (each with approximately a 5 percent share) are all scrambling to maintain sales growth, their respective market shares, and profit margins.

In 2007, the average supermarket had approximately $14 million in annual revenue. Supermarkets with 5 or less stores had approximately $6 million in annual revenue. The largest revenue category segment for supermarkets was perishable foods (accounting for 50 percent of total sales). Nonperishable foods and nonfood items accounted for 30 percent of sales and 20 percent of sales, respectively. Although consumer purchases of "at-home food" is growing, the supermarkets' share of "at-home food" purchases is shrinking. Several research studies have shown that not only are consumers shopping at supermarkets less often (from 71 trips per year to 61), but also the amount of purchases per trip has been reduced. In contrast, both the incidence and amount of grocery shopping have grown for both supercenters and warehouse clubs.

Competitive Factors in a Slow Economy

Competitive factors in the grocery sector have always been directly or indirectly associated with differentiation opportunities. Whole Foods' tremendous growth has been accomplished as it differentiated itself with specialty gourmet product offerings, natural and organic foods, and excellent dialogues with knowledgeable sales personnel. Supercenters have differentiated themselves as "one stop shop" retailers, where a customer can purchase groceries, conduct banking activities, and even purchase concert tickets. Recent differentiation efforts include Kroger's foray into selling gasoline; approximately 700 supermarkets out of 2,500 sell gasoline. SuperValu followed with a partnership with Marathon Oil to sell gas at nearby SuperValu supermarkets.

Another major competitive advantage in the retail grocer sector is being a low-cost provider. Warehouse clubs enable customers to secure excellent values through low rent, low overhead costs, a "no-frills" shopping environment, reduced assortments, and bulk purchasing. Differentiation and cost advantages can sometimes also overlap such as Trader Joe's foreign influenced foods, excellent levels of customer support, and its low prices.

Customer Loyalty Strategies – Lower Prices or Service

The retail grocery sector has always heavily invested to both attract new customers and keep existing customers happy through loyalty programs. Discounts on selected merchandise and special promotions at stores are examples of pricing initiatives to lure new customers. Recent expansion efforts through new store openings (Wal-Mart, Target) or acquisitions (Whole Foods' purchase of Wild Oats, SuperValu's purchase of Albertson's) reflect an effort to address this balance by gaining more new customers through growth (store expansion or acquisition) than are lost to competitors.

The tasks for attracting new customers and keeping current customers is especially difficult since pricing tactics and many merchandise offerings that could potentially differentiate one store from another are especially easy for competitors to copy. This creates a situation where many grocers simply trade customers.

The quest for a loyal customer (an existing customer or a new customer that stays) is based on the economic benefits of loyalty. Professor Frederick Reichheld identified four basic economic benefits that occur when customers remain loyal:

- Loyal customers cost less to serve.
- Loyal customers are usually willing to pay more than other customers (they realize the advantages stores provide for them).
- Loyal customers provide word-of-mouth communication (they don't need to be targeted with the same level of promotion).
- When a loyal customer's purchase power increases, the retailer gains that increase without any special efforts.

A Local Economy's Challenge

This case is based in a Midwest U.S. community that reflects the national economy's sluggish growth, rising costs, and a competitive environment structure with two Kroger stores, a Wal-Mart store, a Carnival Foods store, an Aldi store, a Meijer store, scores of convenience stores, and a Giant Eagle supermarket. In addition, there are two additional Kroger stores, two additional Wal-Mart superstores, and a Sam's Club all within driving distance for local shoppers. The competition for market share in this community is high, and all of the players are using the differentiation and cost-based strategies, although none are clear winners.

A representative from one of the local Kroger stores contacted a professor at a local university and arranged for a retail management class to put together a grocery sector report using both secondary and primary data. Students were asked to collect data that could be used to recommend cost effective retail strategies that maintain and increase customer loyalty. The recommended strategy should be based on the economic benefits of loyalty.

The information gathering activities were directed by this project question: "What is the state of grocery service in our local marketplace relative to important loyalty factors?" The project proceeded based on an information gathering strategy where the secondary data would guide the primary data gathering activities.

Information Gathering

The university information gathering team had several options when selecting useful secondary data. The secondary data search process on the grocery industry focused on business periodicals that report industry data, forecasts, and industry sector survey results. In addition to using online data bases such as Proquest, the student team used Web sites that serve as clearinghouses for marketing research such as www.mediabuyerplanner.com.

In selecting the primary data gathering process, the team examined the feasibility of designing and implementing survey research, conducting several focus groups, or using mystery shopping techniques. Mystery shopping was selected as an appropriate source of primary information on competitive advantage opportunities that contribute to loyalty.

While not a new technique, mystery shopping initially faltered due to its high costs, questions concerning the reliability of the data (the shoppers are not researchers), and its use for employee evaluations. Its resurgence was driven by a number of factors including greater cost control (through combining evaluation of service systems and personnel with merchandise audits that have a high return on investment) and the use of standardized data gathering observation instruments to increase reliability. In addition to traditional retailers, banks and restaurants were increasingly using mystery shopping to identify competitive advantage opportunities.

Research Findings

Secondary Information: Although the team found quite a bit of general information on the state of the grocery sector, it focused on a 2007 survey report by IBM Global Business Services. The survey results defined three shopper profiles based on loyalty: Advocates, Apathetics, and Antagonists. Shoppers who recommend their grocer to others, stick with the store despite competitive offers, and purchase from that store regularly are the most loyal and are identified as "Advocates." "Apathetics" are shoppers with no strong feelings or loyalty to any grocer. Shoppers who have a poor attitude toward their grocer and actively seek to damage the grocer's reputation are identified as "Antagonists." The survey reported that only 23 percent of grocery consumers are Advocates—not a good mark, but it does indicate tremendous opportunities to turn Antagonists and Apathetics into Advocates. This research project found that 79 percent of consumers would commit to a deeper product/service relationship after a satisfying experience.

Word-of-mouth communication was also found to be very important. Thirty-one percent of those consumers who fit the Antagonist profile were reported to tell others of their bad experiences. In addition, 48 percent of Apathetic shoppers reported avoiding a store based on someone else's unsatisfactory experience.

Perhaps the most revealing data from the survey is the difference in service satisfaction between

Advocates and Antagonists in key loyalty building areas. For each of five satisfaction measures:

- Employees are friendly and positive.
- Shoppers are pleased with the service from store employees.
- A grocery store provides a convenient shopping experience.
- Store employees are knowledgeable and attentive.
- Overall, the store is a pleasant and enjoyable place to shop.

The difference in customer satisfaction scores between Advocates and Antagonists was between 50 percent and 56 percent. For example, while 94 percent of the Advocates agreed with the first satisfaction measure ("a grocery store provides a convenient shopping experience"), only 38 percent of the Antagonists agreed with this statement.

Primary Data Collection and Analysis: Using the IBM survey results as a guideline, the university team drafted a mystery shopping checklist that facilitated the observation of grocers in these five satisfaction measures (see bullets above). The checklist used multiple observation areas (i.e., greeting at beginning, during, and at checkout) for four of the five loyalty measures. Overall satisfaction with the shopping experience was a single item response on the checklist.

Accuracy-based measures included bagging of groceries (cold with cold, meats alone, frozen alone, cans with soft foods, etc.). Supplemental areas included the grocer's coffee shop, ticket office, pharmacy, sushi bar, etc. Service counters included meat, deli, bakery, dairy, and produce.

Each mystery shopping observation included one request to locate a merchandise item or service center. In addition to the satisfaction measures, the questionnaire asked for information regarding the store shopped at, the total amount of purchases (in both number of items and dollar amounts), the day and time of shopping, and information on the observer/recorder. The checklist also provided space where the shopper could record any additional observations that occurred during the mystery shopping experience.

Each individual student in the class (25 in number) attended a training session on mystery shopping and was responsible for shopping a grocery store once per week for nine weeks (for a total of 225 mystery shopping observations). The checklists were submitted online to the course Web site each week. Students could conduct the mystery shopping observation while doing their own grocery shopping or accompanying another individual as he or she shopped. Table 1 summarizes the class observations.

Table 1
Mystery Shopping Data Collected Over Two Months

Observations = 1 shopping experience	Kroger 90 shops	Wal-Mart 65 shops	Meijer 35 shops	Carnival 15 shops	Festival 10 shops	Others 10 shops
Employees are friendly and positive Initiated welcome at beginning of shopping	6 initiated out of 90	60 initiated out of 65	5 initiated out of 35	0 initiated out of 15	3 initiated out of 10	0 initiated out of 10
Initiated greeting during shopping	25 of 90	12 of 65	25 of 35	2 of 15	1 of 10	0 of 10
Initiated greeting at checkout	62 of 90	60 of 65	35 of 35	5 of 15	7 of 10	5 of 10
Pleasant shopping experience Aisles/bathroom clean	42 of 90	63 of 65	23 of 35	9 of 15	4 of 10	2 of 10
Temperature comfortable	13 of 90	61 of 65	27 of 35	13 of 15	8 of 10	9 of 10
Courtesy extended ("find everything…" and "thanks for shopping")	22 of 90	31 of 65	28 of 35	7 of 15	3 of 10	2 of 10

Convenience						
Carts available and lot clean	85 of 90	64 of 65	30 of 35	3 of 15	4 of 10	0 of 10
Enough cashier lines open/bagger present	75 of 90	59 of 65	20 of 35	4 of 15	6 of 10	2 of 10
Supplemental service areas staffed	24 of 90	65 of 65	31 of 35	7 of 15	4 of 10	2 of 10
Knowledge/attentive-ness						
Checkout accuracy (number of bags packed incorrectly)	540 of 1,800	585 of 1,300	394 of 525	113 of 150	45 of 50	25 of 30
Directions to merchandise	70 of 90	53 of 65	29 of 35	3 of 15	4 of 10	1 of 10
Service counter help (meat, produce, etc.)	85 of 90	49 of 65	21 of 35	8 of 15	6 of 10	0 of 10
Overall service rated very pleasant	13 of 90	27 of 65	14 of 35	4 of 15	1 of 10	0 of 10

Questions:

1. Can a supermarket obtain both differentiation and cost advantages at the same time? Explain your answer.

2. Describe the pros and cons to using mystery shopping as a data collection technique.

3. Develop specific observational questions to study the five key issues highlighted in Table 1.

4. Develop an appropriate research design that should govern the collection, tabulation, and analysis of mystery shopping data.

5. How can a supermarket turn an Antagonist into an Advocate? ...an Apathetic into an Advocate?

6. Evaluate the implications of Table 1.

SHORT CASES

CASE 1

B&Q

This case was prepared and written by Professors Suzanne Fernie, Fife College of Further and Higher Education, St. Andrews, Scotland; and John Fernie, Heriot-Watt University, Edinburgh, Scotland. Reprinted by permission.

INTRODUCTION

Early in 2005, B&Q (www.diy.com) received unprecedented global publicity when Ellen MacArthur became the fastest person to sail solo around the world in her dual-branded tri-maran B&Q/Castorama. Sponsorship of MacArthur cost £2.5 million a year (about $4.55 million U.S. as of summer 2005), but 18 months of sponsorship brought £5 million worth of publicity to B&Q and Castorama–even before the record-breaking global voyage. Media coverage built brand awareness and paved the way for the global expansion for both retailers.

B&Q had plans for MacArthur to race the old tea-clipper route from Shanghai, China, to London in an attempt to beat a record which had stood since the 19th century. This would build further valuable global brand recognition with the intent of drawing attention to B&Q's rapid expansion of its home improvement stores in China.

Growth of B&Q
Founded by Richard Block and David Quayle in 1969, B&Q is a United Kingdom chain of do-it-yourself and home improvement stores. By 1980, when the company was acquired by Woolworths, there were 39 B&Q stores located in a variety of locations including old movie theaters and warehouses. Rapid expansion continued during the 1980s including the acquisition of the Scottish do-it-yourself chain, Dodge City. By the end of the decade, B&Q, with 280 stores, had become part of the Kingfisher Group, along with Woolworths, Superdrug, and Comet.

During the 1990s, B&Q developed larger format stores that were branded as B&Q Warehouse. These stores were over 100,000 square feet in size and complemented the company's portfolio of smaller stores called B&Q Supercentres. There was also a focus on international expansion, with the first overseas B&Q store opening in Taiwan. The following year, B&Q entered the Chinese market with its first store in Shanghai. This was the chain's largest store at that time.

In 2001, B&Q's online store (http://www.diy.com) opened in response to rising ownership of home computers in the United Kingdom and the increased use of the Internet to research and purchase goods and services. At the time, B&Q had plans to expand its Web site to offer online sales of most of the 40,000 products already available through the B&Q catalog. In the long term, the site was expected to sell between 60,000 and 70,000 products–more than that available in B&Q stores. As of 2005, B&Q had become the world's third largest do-it-yourself chain with over 300 stores in the United Kingdom and an additional 50 stores in other countries.

Expansion in China

B&Q has been enthusiastic about the potential of the Chinese market. Its Beijing stores alone serve 13 million potential customers in a growing home improvement market caused by the opening up of the housing market. The Chinese government offered special concessions to retailers seeking to expand their operations in China. For example, the Beijing Commerce Commission and Beijing Finance Bureau offered discount interest rates for bank loans for retailers that opened franchise supermarkets and convenience stores in Beijing.

B&Q's outlet in Jinsjii, Beijing, which opened in October 2003, was the company's 14th store in China. At 250,000 square feet in size, it was the largest B&Q in the world, and twice the size of an average B&Q warehouse. Two additional B&Q stores opened the following year in Shuangjing and Laiguangying.

Until December 2004, B&Q was forced to form strategic alliances with local companies to operate in the Chinese market; B&Q was also not allowed to open more than three stores in any Chinese city. As of January 2005, the Chinese government relaxed the legislation governing the expansion of foreign retailers. The new law meant that B&Q could operate without the need for a foreign partner and that it could open an unlimited number of stores in any Chinese city.

The Attraction of the Chinese Home Improvement Market

As living standards in China improved, interior decorating became an immensely popular activity in key Chinese market areas. In the past, household improvements in China had been largely the responsibility of the state, with a focus on providing adequate shelter for most of the population and the reduction of overcrowding in urban areas. Since 1980, about 20 percent of the public housing in Chinese cities had been upgraded. As better public housing was being developed, consumers' income rose, creating higher expectations of housing quality. The Chinese government also began to sell off state-owned housing as a means of generating a large group of homeowners in the larger cities. This trend is expected to continue throughout China.

Home ownership is expected to grow rapidly in China. In China, only 1.6 percent of people (20 million) owned their own homes in 2004, in comparison with 68 percent of the population in both the United States and the United Kingdom. With a Chinese population of 1.2 billion, the potential and attraction of the home improvement market was clear.

Computer ownership and Internet access has also experienced rapid growth in China. As of 2003, nearly 80 million Chinese had access to the Internet, a figure up 30 percent from the previous year. Growth in use of broadband was even higher, increasing opportunities for the growth of online sales.

While B&Q's Beijing stores stock the same building products and power tools as stores in the United Kingdom, the Beijing stores had more emphasis on design and installation services. Since do-it-yourself is less established in China than the United Kingdom, Chinese customers are more likely to buy goods bundled with the services of a professional installer. Also, since new apartments in China are also commonly sold as shells, there is high demand for professionals to install wiring, plumbing, and flooring.

Competition in the Chinese Home Improvement Market

While B&Q was the only United Kingdom-based home improvement chain in Beijing in 2003, it still faced tough competition. German home improvement retailer, OBI, opened in Beijing, and B&Q faced direct competition from Chinese home improvement retailers such as Orient Home and The Home World. These retailers possessed sophisticated buying, logistics, and marketing capabilities. The Home World planned to open 8 stores in the Beijing area by 2006. Another domestic home improvement retailer with national aspirations, Shanghai's Home Mart, had established a presence in Beijing by 2004 and planned to have up to 50 stores by 2005. Other leading international retailers, such as Wal-Mart and Auchan, had opened Beijing stores and sold selected home improvement items. Despite intensified domestic and international competition, B&Q intends to establish a market lead in China–in 2004, it had 18 stores nationwide with plans for 75 B&Q stores by 2008.

Problems in Europe

Like many other United Kingdom retailers, Kingfisher's concentration on overseas developments appeared to take its toll on its United Kingdom and French operations. Although Kingfisher owned 262 stores across the world (excluding its 300+ B&Q United Kingdom stores), its international operations generated only 10 percent of its profits and its United Kingdom sales experienced poor growth–only 0.6 percent in the final 3 months of 2004. Some of its B&Q stores were showing evidence of neglect and poor management, resulting in out-of-stocks and disappointing sales. For example, same store sales at B&Q fell by 1.2 percent in 2004. In France, Castorama was experiencing similar problems with a decrease in same-store sales of 0.9 percent.

As with Marks and Spencer in the 1990s, the retailer's focus on its international expansion has meant that response to changing markets in the United Kingdom and France had been slow. This could significantly undermine the positive publicity gained through media coverage of MacArthur's achievements and jeopardize B&Q's international expansion objectives.

Questions:

1. Assess the market potential of the Chinese market for home improvement goods using Web-based secondary data sources.

2. Describe how market saturation ratios can measure whether Beijing is understored, overstored, or saturated.

3. Identify the pros and cons of B&Q's using strategic alliances with local companies to operate in the Chinese market versus developing the Chinese market on its own.

4. How can B&Q assure that its domestic and French operations will not be neglected as it pursues opportunities in China?

CASE 2

Bari's Department Store: Gross Margin Blues

This case was prepared and written by Professor Doreen Burdalski, Albright College. Reprinted by permission.

Bari's is a moderately priced, family-owned regional department store chain that currently operates 30 stores throughout Pennsylvania, New Jersey, and Delaware. The company is very financially conservative and historically has opened one to two new stores per year.

Bari's assortment consists of 70 percent soft line and 30 percent hard line merchandise. Sixty percent of the brand mix consists of manufacturer brands such as Levi's, Carter's, and BVD. The balance of its merchandise is private label. The chain's overall assortment policy is wide and deep.

Bari's competition includes national department store and mass merchandise retailers such as Sears, Kohl's, and Target, as well as Boscov's, another regional family-run department store. Bari's also faces significant competition from locally-owned clothing specialty stores. Bari's advertises weekly using full-page ads in local newspapers. It also conducts a small amount of television advertising during peak sales periods such as Christmas and Mother's Day.

Bari's prides itself on each branch store's maintaining strong local ties to its communities through supporting fundraising activities for local schools and churches and local sports teams. Bari's also emphasizes customer service. Bari's employees are trained and motivated to assist the customer. Most shoppers would agree with the comment that Bari's is a clean and friendly store.

Ashley Brown, the junior jeans buyer for Bari's, joined the company five years ago after working for Sears for almost a decade. While the junior jeans department at Bari's accounts for 3.8 percent of the store's total sales, it is considered an important profit center for the store. The junior jeans department last year had a gross margin of 38.7 percent. Although the department's gross margin has been declining over the past three years, it is still higher than the store's overall gross margin of 34.2 percent. Brown attributes the declining gross margin to rising jean costs, particularly on the basic branded products.

See Table 1 for a vendor analysis that contains sales and maintained margin data for the junior jeans department by vendor for the years 2006, 2007, and 2008. The department is 60 percent basic (staple) jeans and 40 percent fashion jeans. Vendors A, B, and C supply predominantly basic jeans (occasionally Brown will purchase a fashion style or two from these vendors) and Vendors D, E, F, and G supply fashion jeans. Each vendor supplies point-of-purchase marketing materials (such as graphic signs, size indicators, and size strips) that are integrated into the department's fixtures and walls.

Brown uses a competition-oriented pricing strategy. She aims to be at or below the competition on comparable products. Prices in the department range from $24.99 to $49.99. All of Bari's basic 5-pocket jean vendor's jeans use the opening price point of $24.99. Rising costs for jeans have made it increasingly difficult for Bari's to maintain the opening price point and continue to maintain the department's gross margin.

Brown is now in the position of having to place jeans orders for the upcoming back-to-school season. She has recently been notified that most of her jean vendors have raised prices on all of their fall goods. Due to the current recession and the fact that Brown's larger competitors also carry the same brands, she does not feel that she can raise the retail price on the basic jeans this back-to-school season. This will continue to erode her department's gross profits.

At a recent trade show, Brown met a jeans manufacturer that produces jeans and other clothing items in Mexico. Brown has judged the quality and fit of this manufacturer's products as outstanding. The manufacturer agreed to make its jeans as a Bari's private label. The cost of the basic style would be approximately 20 percent lower than a comparable manufacturer's brand. While Brown tried to negotiate with her divisional merchandise manager (DMM) for extra space for this good, the DMM told Brown this was not possible, since the jeans department's gross margin has been declining.

Questions

1.   Interpret Table 1.

2.   How can Bari's increase the gross margin for its manufacturer brands? … for its private label brands?

3.   What are the relative advantages of stocking a large proportion of private brands for Bari's? …the disadvantages?

4.   What do you recommend that Ashley Brown do when placing orders for the fall?

Table 1
Bari's Department Stores
Junior Jeans Department
Vendor Analysis
2006-2008

Vendor	Sales 2006	% of Sales	Maintained Markup % 2006	Sales 2007	% of Sales	Maintained Markup % 2007	Sales 2008
A	$ 5,750,000	25%	37.00%	$ 6,037,500	25%	36.50%	$ 5,750,000
B	$ 4,600,000	20%	36.00%	$ 5,554,500	23%	36.10%	$ 6,250,000
C	$ 4,600,000	20%	35.80%	$ 3,622,500	15%	35.00%	$ 3,250,000
D	$ 3,450,000	15%	40.20%	$ 3,622,500	15%	40.10%	$ 3,750,000
E	$ 1,840,000	8%	40.50%	$ 2,415,000	10%	40.80%	$ 3,000,000
F	$ 1,610,000	7%	40.30%	$ 1,690,500	7%	40.50%	$ 1,750,000
G	$ 1,150,000	5%	39.50%	$ 1,207,500	5%	40.00%	$ 1,250,000
Total	$23,000,000			$24,150,000			$25,000,000

CASE 3

Basically Bagels: Promotion Mix Planning to Grow and Strengthen a Business

This case was prepared and written by Professor Anne Heineman Batory, Wilkes University, Pennsylvania; and Professor Stephen S. Batory, Bloomsburg University, Pennsylvania. Reprinted by permission.

Ron and Kathy Lieberman decided to open a bagel bakery/restaurant after being unable to find freshly-baked bagels and fresh appetizing supplies (such as cut-to-order smoked white fish and homemade cream cheese) near their home. After more than three years of planning, they opened their store, Basically Bagels, in a Wilkes-Barre, Pennsylvania, suburb. Although Ron and Kathy both knew the retail site they chose was poor (in terms of pedestrian and vehicle traffic and road visibility), they chose it based on the low rent. The Liebermans realized they would need to devise and enact an effective promotional program to generate and sustain store traffic at the site.

The initial promotional strategy for the store's grand opening fully met its goals. The local cable TV station and the local newspaper provided excellent coverage. As a result, the store was very busy during its first three weeks of operation. Unfortunately, sales soon slackened off. The owners attributed this to two factors: a reduction in the novelty effect for a new store and the store's air-conditioning system being inadequate during the hot and humid summer season.

For two years, the Liebermans' attempts to expand sales were unsuccessful. This was despite running coupons (such as "Buy 12 bagels, get 6 free") and using the shop as a broadcast site for a popular local radio station. However, the coupons did not generate added revenues because most redeemers were current customers. While the Liebermans were initially excited about the on-site broadcast that featured a popular disk jockey, it had virtually no effect on store traffic or sales.

Two key events occurred during the third year of Basically Bagels' operation that led to the successful turnaround of the firm. First, the Liebermans began selling a line of gift baskets (as an alternative to fruit baskets), besides their usual bagels and appetizing products. The gift baskets consisted of special bagels (with a long shelf life), cream cheese spreads, specialty coffees, and other gourmet products housed in an attractive wicker basket. The baskets were promoted via a one-page, three-fold flyer that was mailed to community residents and businesses.

The second positive event was a bartering agreement negotiated between the Liebermans and WKRZ, the area's leading radio station. Through this agreement, the radio station received bagel baskets and other merchandise (primarily for use in listener contests) as full payment for Basically Bagels' spot advertising. The long-term use of these ads and contests resulted in continued reinforcement of the store and its high-quality products.

After being at their original location for over eight years, the Liebermans still advertise on WKRZ and participate in contests aimed at the station's listeners. Basically Bagels has also begun to use local cable TV advertising (with spot commercials on general news and business

42

news programs) and to run a commercial on an early-morning news program of a local TV network affiliate.

Although Basically Bagels no longer offers coupons or price promotions, it gives its customers its own form of a "Baker's Dozen" (14 bagels for the cost of a dozen) to increase sales volume. It has instituted a frequent-buyer club for specialty coffee and bagel products to raise consumer loyalty. In this program, customers receive the eleventh cup of coffee or the eleventh specialty bagel free of charge. Recently, Basically Bagels expanded its hours of operation by having an "After Hours" evening cafe with specialty coffees and pastries.

Basically Bagels has begun to refine the promotion of its gift baskets. The gift basket catalog is now a glossy, full-color catalog that is professionally prepared. And the gift baskets are to be marketed on the firm's new Web site. With these promotional vehicles, Basically Bagels plans to sell its gift baskets beyond its normal trading area. Basically Bagels also now promotes its bagel baskets as a bereavement token in tactful ads placed in the obituary section of the town's paper.

The success of Basically Bagels has not gone unnoticed. Several competitors, including both local bakers and units of nationally-based franchises, have entered the Wilkes-Barre suburban market. Ron and Kathy Lieberman know that it is time again to re-examine their store's overall promotional strategy.

Questions:

1.   Evaluate Basically Bagels' overall promotional strategy.

2.   What additional promotional media should now be considered? Explain your answer.

3.   What is the role of public relations for Basically Bagels?

4.   How should Ron and Kathy revise their promotional strategy based on the emergence of competitors?

CASE 4

Beverages and More!: Devising and Enacting an Integrated Retail Strategy

This case was prepared and written by Professor Howard W. Combs, San Jose State University, California. Reprinted by permission.

Founded in 1994, Beverages and More! is a rapidly growing and successful chain of category killer beverage and gourmet snack food stores in the San Francisco area. The heart of each of its 18,000-square-foot stores is the superior wine and beer selection.

While a traditional California supermarket carries 30 or so Chardonnay wines, Beverages and More! carries over 300 (from a variety of vineyards and vintages). Wines account for 40 percent of the chain's total sales. And beers and spirits comprise another 40 percent. The typical Beverages and More! store stocks over 300 microbrews, 300 imported beers, and over 1,200 spirits. Gourmet food, nonalcoholic beverages, and general merchandise make up 15 percent of sales; the other 5 percent is from cigars. Four-foot-high glass cases equipped with humidifiers display the cigars near each store entrance. Most of them are imported from the Caribbean.

Several new product categories are being added to the Beverages and More! product mix. These include some 500 types of cheeses, fresh pasta, olives, deli salads, dips, and gourmet deli meats. A test of frozen appetizers and desserts is in process. These new items are expected to boost the proportion of overall revenues attributed to food to around 25 percent.

Prices at Beverages and More! have remained relatively low due to the chain's low purchase costs and low overhead. Because the firm purchases huge amounts of its goods, it is able to take advantage of quantity discounts and its buying clout with vendors. Furthermore, Beverages and More! generates additional savings by insisting that most vendors deliver their goods directly to the chain's stores, as opposed to a distribution center. Direct store delivery reduces costs due to the elimination of certain warehousing and shipping expenses.

The chain's primary market is 35- to 54-year-olds, who are affluent and college educated. Males presently account for 60 percent of the firm's total revenues. In contrast, 90 percent of the customers of a typical liquor store customer are male. Beverages and More! appeals both to consumers who shop the store regularly and seek a wide selection and low prices, and those who visit the stores to stock up for parties and holiday gatherings. The average transaction size at a Beverages and More! store is over $30.

Beverages and More! recently launched Club Bev, a frequent shopper program. With Club Bev, each purchase by a member is scanned; and the chain then enters the information into its data base. The data base is used to develop targeted newsletters that reflect individual consumer purchase histories. Thus, the newsletter for a cigar smoker has a different editorial content than a newsletter oriented toward a cheese buyer.

Even though the chain is very young, Beverages and More! has ambitious expansion plans. It hopes to enter other areas of California in the near future. After that, it will consider other markets—possibly the East Coast.

Questions:

1. What are the competitive advantages and disadvantages of Beverages and More! in comparison with traditional beverage stores? In comparison with traditional gourmet food stores?

2. Do you think that Beverages and More!'s retailing strategy is well integrated? Explain your answer.

3. Present a five-year plan for Beverages and More! to expand into other regions of the United States. What potential risks does it face? How would you overcome them?

4.   Describe a customer-service vertical retail audit for Beverages and More!

CASE 5

The Burj Al Arab: Measuring Guest Satisfaction at the World's Only 7-Star Hotel

This case was prepared and written by Professor Michael Luthy, Bellarmine University. Reprinted by permission.

Designed to resemble a sail on a sailboat blowing in the wind, the Burj Al Arab hotel, part of the Jumeirah Group, stands over 1,000 feet and dominates the Dubai coastline in the United Arab Emirates. The hotel contains 202 duplex suites, ranging from 1,800 to 8,400 square feet in size on its 27 floors. In addition to dining and living areas, each suite contains an office area complete with laptop, Internet access, private fax, printer, and copier. Each suite also has a 42-inch plasma screen television with video on demand capabilities, a DVD player, 93 cable channels, and two hotel information channels, and a hot tub. For those with more specific requirements, there is even a pillow menu with a range of 13 pillows and quilts for the guest to choose among.

Other hotel amenities include a spa and health club with treatment rooms, hydrotherapy baths, steam rooms, Jacuzzis, a squash court, two fully-equipped fitness studios, and an aerobics floor. Within the hotel itself are a number of restaurants and lounges:
- Al Mahara – an award-winning seafood restaurant accessible by a three-minute virtual submarine voyage. Al Mahara's aquarium is visible throughout the restaurant.
- Al Muntaha – located at 650 feet above the Arabian Gulf. This restaurant offers Mediterranean cuisine.
- Junsui – an authentic Asian restaurant with 12 live cooking stations and 45 specialized chefs.
- Al Iwan – offering the finest Arabian hospitality.
- Majlis Al Bahar – a casual alfresco restaurant serving Mediterranean specialties with spectacular views of the gulf and Burj Al Arab.
- Sahn Eddar – located at the base of the world's tallest atrium. This restaurant offers light foods, as well as afternoon tea.
- Juna Lounge – a stylish and intimate lounge offering a fine selection of cigars.
- Skyview Bar – located adjacent to Al Muntaha.
- Bab Al Yam – a café restaurant with a relaxing atmosphere that enables guests to see stunning views of the Arabian Gulf.

To assess the satisfaction of its guests, the Burj Al Arab provides them with a guest satisfaction questionnaire at check-in and asks them to either fill it out before they leave or to mail it to the hotel when they get home. In contrast, other hotels typically determine guest satisfaction through providing a questionnaire at check out, or through mailing or E-mailing the questionnaire to one's home. The Burj Al Arab uses a two-sided form that asks the identical questions in English and in Arabic.

Questions:

1. Discuss the pros and cons of giving the guest satisfaction questionnaire at a guest's arrival versus at departure.

2. What are the difficulties in designing and interpreting a questionnaire in multiple languages for worldwide guests?

3. Describe the differences in questionnaire design for a luxury hotel versus a traditional Holiday Inn.

4. Design a 15-item questionnaire to ascertain guest satisfaction for the Burj Al Arab.

CASE 6

Calle Ocho: A Yearly Festival in Miami

This case was prepared and written by Professor Jonathan N. Goodrich, Florida International University. Reprinted by permission.

INTRODUCTION

Calle Ocho ("Eight Street" in Spanish) is an annual one-day street festival/carnival held in Miami, Florida on the first or second Sunday in March. The festival takes placed on 8th Street in Miami, from about 4th Avenue to 27th Avenue (an area about a mile long). This area is part of South Florida's historic Cuban community, known as Little Havana.

Calle Ocho began in 1978 as a celebration of the Cuban culture. Today, it is a celebration by people from all walks of life and of ethnic diversity. Calle Ocho is characterized by dancing, loud music, merriment, celebration, eating, and drinking. Among its features are dancing in the street to the beat of different kinds of music (e.g., merengue, soca, reggae) by over 100 Latin musicians and bands, as well as the sale of all kinds of food, drinks, and arts and crafts by over 200 retailers.

In 2005, an estimated one million people participated in Calle Ocho. The annual economic impact of the festival has been estimated at between $10 million and $15 million. This is reflected in the increased sales at restaurants, hotel/motel accommodations, airline tickets, car rentals, as well as direct purchases at the festival.

Background
Some people come to Calle Ocho for the tremendous variety of ethnic food (sold at food stands, booths, and shops). Others come for the music played by some 100 mobile and stationary bands

on stage, or to listen to well-known (e.g., Julio Iglesias, Gloria Estefan, Willy Chirino) and aspiring singers. Still others come simply to relax, have a good time, and people watch. Many companies, such as Coca-Cola, Bacardi, Procter & Gamble, McDonald's, Bank of America, and American Express, advertise, give away samples of products, sell goods and services, and gather data for market research studies.

Products

Most of the 200 street vendors along S.W. 8th Street concentrate on selling food and beverages. Music CD vendors generally concentrate on well-known artists, and cover the musical gamut of salsa, soca, reggae, merengue, calypso, hip-hop, Latin rhythms, and ballads. Some street vendors feature paintings, sculptures, jewelry, leather goods, and cigars and cigarettes.

Price

There is a wide range of price points for the products sold at Calle Ocho. See Table 1.

Table 1
Sample of Product Prices

Musical CDs	$15 – $20 each
T-shirts	$10 – $15 each
Beer	$ 4 – $ 5 per can
Soft drinks	$ 3 per can/bottle
Hamburgers	$ 5
Hot Dogs	$ 3
Plate of food (fish, chicken, steak, or ribs, rice and peas, salad)	$10 – $15
Water	$ 3 per bottle
Ice cream cones	$ 2
Paintings	$50 – $300
Watches	$40 – $200
Leather goods (belts, handbags)	$10 – $100

Other Carnivals

Calle Ocho is certainly not the only street carnival in the world. There are many others in the United States (e.g., in New Orleans) and other countries, especially during the summer. Other street carnivals are popular in Canada, Mexico, Brazil, Argentina, Trinidad, Jamaica, Hawaii, and parts of Africa. These carnivals generally have several things in common: dancing, a party atmosphere, food and liquor, the celebration of a culture, the sale of arts and crafts, and food.

Questions:

1. How is retailing reflected at Calle Ocho?

2. What do well-known companies, such as Bank of America, Coca-Cola, Procter & Gamble, and McDonalds often do at Calle Ocho?

3.   Write a paper about two other carnivals. Secure data about these carnivals from a Web search. Compare the two carnivals in question to Calle Ocho.

4.   Develop a promotional program for publicizing Calle Ocho to New York City-based tourists.

CASE 7

Cook 'N Store–Bringing It All Together

This case was prepared and written by Professor Neill Crowley, St. Joseph's University, Philadelphia, Pennsylvania. Reprinted by permission.

Cook 'N Store is a multi-channel retailer that sells a full line of kitchen appliances, utensils, and cookware, as well as home storage and organizing accessories through its catalog, Web, and store-based operations. The business began fifteen years ago as a catalog-based operation that sold a broad and deep assortment of kitchen accessories, cooking utensils, and cookware through mail order. Over the years, additional lines of kitchenware and household organizers were added. And seven years ago, the retailer launched its Web page. The Web page complemented the catalog business since it enabled Cook 'N Store to:

- Change its product mix in real time by adding and deleting items. Some of these items are shipped by vendors directly to the retailer's customers. This process enables Cook 'N Store to dramatically increase its product offerings with little or no additional inventory.
- Interact with customers via E-mail.
- Change prices according to demand and competitive forces.
- Use video and audio in merchandise presentations.
- Reduce costs associated with the printing and mailing of catalogs.
- Highlight special purchases and closeout stock that are available in limited quantities. This merchandise would not be suitable for promotion through catalogs due to their limited availability.

Within the last four years, Cook 'N Store opened ten stores in lifestyle centers. Unlike huge regional shopping centers, lifestyle centers are characterized by a focus on apparel, home products, and music retailers, as well as restaurants. These centers appeal to shoppers who do not want to walk through a huge regional shopping center, who have a more defined shopping need, and who want to combine shopping and dining on one trip. All of the stores have met the retailer's expectations and Cook 'N Store had initiated plans with two major developers of lifestyle centers to be included in their next ten projects.

While all three of Cook 'N Store's businesses (i.e., catalog, Web, stores) were individually doing well, the retailer's top management was continuously concerned with how these three businesses could be better integrated so as to achieve cost savings and synergy for the chain.

Questions:

1. Identify the chief advantages and disadvantages of each of Cook 'N Store's retail formats.

2. Should Cook 'N Store charge the same price for the same merchandise in each format? Explain your answer.

3. Discuss possible sources of cost savings due to Cook 'N Store's operating multiple formats.

4. Describe how the three retail formats can be better integrated.

CASE 8

Cross-Cultural Menu Design: Accommodating Tourists at an Icelandic Steakhouse

This case was prepared and written by Professor Michael Luthy, Bellarmine University. Reprinted by permission.

In a country known for fish and lamb products, Icelandic steakhouses represent a special destination for the local population, as well as a "taste of home" for tourists from countries where beef is a more significant part of their diet. Without significant domestic cattle production, beef products must be shipped in to an island country located just below the Arctic Circle. As a result of high transportation costs, the price of steak in Iceland is substantially higher than one would find in the United States or many European countries.

Hereford Steikhus (a steakhouse) is located at Laugarvegur 53b in the heart of Reykjavik, the capital city of Iceland, on the old city's main shopping street. Reykjavik is a very vibrant city, beyond what many would expect. It could easily be mistaken for other European capitals with extensive shopping opportunities, diverse cultural offerings, and an energetic nightlife environment. The Reykjavik metropolitan area is home to a population of 180,000 in a country with just over 300,000 people. Although just two hours by plane from England and five hours from the American east coast, Iceland's current annual tourist visitation rate is equal to the country's population and is projected to grow to 1,000,000 by 2010.

The challenge for Hereford, as it is for any upscale restaurant, is how to deliver the dining experience—meeting or exceeding the expectations of its patrons. Hereford's situation is made more problematic given the implications of a large tourist component to its business. If one were to limit the potential clientele to just those from the United States and Western Europe, the restaurant would still have to consider the barriers associated with a half-dozen foreign languages. Other cultural differences would also have to be considered.

Upon arriving at Hereford and being welcomed, the host/hostess sits the party at a table and takes their drink order. Each person is given an order card, as well as a menu. Menus are available in a umber of languages. To avoid confusion, menu options are listed in a multiple-choice format. This enables a tourist to choose among preparation (from bleu to well done for steaks), and potato, butter, sauce, and side dish options. The English language version of the menu is alongside the Icelandic language version. (Icelandic is a North Germanic-based Nordic language). Items like a T-bone steak and shish kabob are also featured in pictures to avoid further confusion.

Other restaurants with large tourist populations have faced similar issues. For example, many tourist destination restaurants with large foreign tourist populations help resolve language and tourist issues by:
- showing pictures of popular menu items.
- using multi-language menus.
- hiring wait staff that are multilingual.
- listing menu prices in U.S. dollars, as well as common currencies.
- showing all foreign credit cards that are accepted.
- toning down spicy dishes.
- training the wait staff to explain use of local ingredients, as well as food preparation.
- replacing dishes that tourists cannot eat.
- explaining how special dishes are served.
- explaining customary tipping procedures on the bill.

Question:

1.   Develop a marketing plan for a tourist destination restaurant to accommodate a large tourist target market. Assume that the tourists come from around the world, may not understand the native language, and are unfamiliar with local ingredients and preparation.

CASE 9

Custom Ski Pants: New Technology on the Selling Floor

This case was prepared and written by Professor Doris H. Kincade, Virginia Tech University, Virginia; and Professor Ginger Woodard, East Carolina University, North Carolina. Reprinted by permission.

In June, Randy Barbar, the active sports-athletic wear buyer for Specialty Sportswear stores, met with Sam Tando, the sales representative of the Fast Track Ski Products company, to discuss the upcoming Winter line. For a change, Tando had a really new product line including a computer kiosk with a body-scanning booth. The equipment was called the Custom Fit Unit (CFU) and was designed to measure a person and take information about color and style to create an order for custom-made ski pants. Measurements and color/style preference would be transmitted directly from the store to the Fast Track Ski Products sewing plants and each pair of custom pants, when completed, would be directly shipped to the customer. From order date to shipping should take only a few days. The customer would have custom-made pants in less than one week.

Barbar knew that custom-made ski pants had great potential. With more and more people becoming active with winter sports, fitting all body types with those tight-shaped ski pants was impossible. As Barbar listened to Tando's sales pitch, images of piles of messy stock, hundreds of returns of pants with broken seams and sprung knees, and lines of dissatisfied customers began to disappear. Instead, she envisioned the ringing of the cash register, happy employees, and smiling customers. After watching a video of a customer using the CFU and a few more minutes of listening to Tando, Barbar was enchanted with the idea of body scanning and custom-fit ski pants.

As part of the negotiations for the product line, Sam Tando offered two deals. Option A required the Specialty Sportswear stores to make a deposit with Fast Track of $22,000 per store to receive the CFU. The deposit would be returned, minus some service fees, when sales of the custom pants passed $80,000 per store. In return for the deposit, each Specialty Sportswear store would receive a full installation of the equipment and 320 hours of training for employees in each store. Option B required a guarantee of $45,000 in sales per store, no deposit, and one day (8 hours) of training for each store manager.

Randy Barbar immediately chose Option B. Lack of cash flow and a belief that the custom pants would be an immediate sales success fueled her decision. Knowing the number of ski pants sold in one winter season, Barbar was confident that the guaranteed minimum sales amount would be easily surpassed. As for training, she thought, "How hard could it be to punch a few buttons on the computer screen and stand in a dark booth? Besides, the stores had already spent $1.5 million on training sales staff on the new electronic cash registers and everyone knows about computers, right?" Barbar signed the Option B contract.

In mid-September, a CFU was delivered to 10 Specialty Sportswear stores. Each store manager received the eight hours of training during the last week in September. The CFU was introduced to the sales staff at the following Monday morning staff meeting. The corporate plan at Specialty Sportswear was that each manager would train one assistant manager who would be responsible for the kiosk and booth and would do any additional training of sales staff as needed. During the first of October, the manager in Store #1 left the company, and the manager from Store #5 was promoted to a district position. The assistant manager in Store #1 was promoted to manager, and the assistant manager in Store #3 was transferred to Store #5 as manager. With the Founder's Day sale on October 8th and the series of absences due to the flu, no training was done for assistant managers or sales staff.

The sales staff was told that they would not receive the usual 10 percent commission on sales generated by the CFU, but would instead receive a 3 percent commission. The reasons for the lower commission were the reduced time in stock handling and the reduced time in bagging the purchases. Sales staff were told to greet customers looking at the CFU with the usual store greeting but to assist customers only if they had specific questions. The managers decided in their quarterly meeting that the custom process with body measurements was a personal issue and that too much attention by the sales staff would be embarrassing to the customers.

Early November officially starts the peak sales period of skiwear. Although the region had had a few snowfalls and plenty of cold weather, sales of ski pants through the CFU were minimal. The Specialty Sportswear stores had included a promotion about the CFU and the new custom-made ski pants in the bills for their store charge customers. The promotion included an explanation of the process and a coupon for $10 off the purchase of a pair of custom ski pants or $5 off the purchase of any new skiwear item in the store. Throughout the stores, 100 coupons had been collected but the register transactions showed that none of them were used for purchase of the custom pants.

In early December, Randy Barbar rechecked the sales of the custom pants relative to the other ski pants. Sales of the regular pants were on schedule with previous seasons. Barbar was alarmed to find that the custom pants had sales that added up to one-third of the necessary $45,000. She knew that fast action was required. The week after Thanksgiving was past and with it, the maximum sales potential time for the entire season. If sales of the custom pants did not double in the next two weeks, she was doomed. Instead of happy customers and ringing cash registers, Barbar had visions of unpaid bills and her boss yelling. Her first thought was to blame the sales staff. They were probably ignoring the customers and were not pushing the CFU. She thought that anytime a product line failed to sell, the sales staff could be blamed for the poor sales performance. "They are the people on the front line. Why don't they make people buy the products that I so carefully select?" She shook her head in wonder.

Overnight, Barbar devised a plan. She thought, "I will catch those lazy sales staffers. I'll send out the secret shoppers." She talked with security and hired two people that were recommended as secret shoppers. Each was assigned five stores and given a charge card with instructions to shop for and order custom pants in each of the five stores. A report to Barbar was due in two days.

On the morning of December 6th, the two reports were stacked neatly in the center of Barbar's desk. Armed with a cup of coffee and sweet roll, she began to read. Store #1 was the flagship store for the company. The report was dismal. The secret shopper had found an out-of-order sign taped to the computer screen. When the shopper asked a sales staff employee about the CFU, the reply had been vague and noncommittal, something about the buttons not working since the computer was installed. The story for Store #2 was similar. The secret shopper had tried to use the computer but found that the order form was hard to read and the program had no way to correct errors so her address, which should have been 123 Smith Lane, was 231 Lane Street. She doubted that the package would ever reach her and was not sure that the order had really been transmitted. The tale about Store #5 was even worse. The secret shopper thought she had been shocked when she pushed the button to start the scanning process. When she called out for help, nobody came. After she came out of the booth, she approached a sales staff employee and complained but was told that the sales staff could not assist with the personal aspects of the fitting process.

Randy Barbar put down the report. Her sweet roll was untouched and her coffee was getting cold. She held her head in her hands and wondered what she should do. What had gone wrong?

Who should she call and what could be done to salvage this disaster?

Questions:

1.   What were the pros and cons of each original option to the retailer?

2.   What training methods should have been used? Why? Who should have received the minimal training that was provided with Option B?

3.   How do you train and motivate sales personnel to help the customer when their commission on these sales has been cut from 10 percent to 3 percent?

4.   How should sales personnel have been supervised to assure that sales on the CFU would be achieved?

5.   Should the buyer have the authority to make this type of decision above for a company? What organizational format would have helped to work through these problems before they occurred?

CASE 10

Deep Water Diving

This case was prepared and written by Professor Michele M. Granger, Southwest Missouri State University. Reprinted by permission.

As the buyers of The Clothes Horse are seated in the conference room, the new merchandise manager of ladies' apparel, Carl Bedell, is sharing both his assessment of the chain store's current marketing strategies and his suggestions to improve the company's bottom line through more effective merchandising techniques. Mr. Bedell believes that the merchandise assortment has been too fragmented and too diverse in the past. He states that the buyers have been overly cautious by purchasing small quantities of an excessive number of styles from an overabundance of vendors. "The breadth of the inventory has been too extreme," he asserts. "The resulting stock," Bedell continues, "looks like an end-of-the-year closeout at the beginning of a new season." He recommends that the buying staff jointly determine important seasonal trends in advance and take a stand on these looks through more in-depth purchases. He explains that the customer decision-making process is simplified with more consistent stock. "When the consumer sees a clear fashion statement in quantity, she concludes that she must have that look to be fashionable," Bedell summarizes. He adds that an inventory with greater depth makes visual merchandising and advertising efforts clearer and more effective. Finally, he suggests that quantity purchases give the buyer more negotiating power with the reduced number of chosen vendors.

Virginia Nelson is the misses' swimwear buyer for The Clothes Horse. She has been a buyer at the store for the past ten years. Although she likes Carl, she is wary of his new approach to merchandising the store. Nelson suspects that Bedell's merchandising philosophy is a result of his years of working with mass-merchandising chains, rather than specialty store organizations. Because of her long-term experience with The Clothes Horse, Virginia Nelson believes that her customer is extremely selective and does not want to see others coming and going in the same garment. "This will be a turnoff to our customers. It's for a mass-marketing operation, not for a specialty store," she thinks. She decides to continue writing her orders the way she always has, but she now must receive approval from the new merchandise manager before actually placing an order. Additionally, Nelson thinks about the manufacturers that she has used for her department over the past decade. Each one, she decides, fills an important niche in the total swimwear stock.

Mr. Bedell slowly reviews the stock of orders that Nelson has prepared and then leans back in his chair. "Virginia, you must not have heard what I said about in-depth purchasing. I see nothing in this pile of orders that reflects a major trend statement. You will need to revise these before I can approve them," he declares. Nelson leaves Bedell's office in frustration.

Questions:

1. If you were in Virginia Nelson's position, what would you do next?

2. What alternatives should Nelson consider? Identify specific criteria to evaluate vendors.

3. If you were in Mr. Bedell's position, what would you do to convince Virginia Nelson that in-depth purchasing is a successful strategy for The Clothes Horse?

4. As the merchandise manager, what specific directions can you give the buyers to implement this merchandising strategy?

CASE 11

Dogwood Kennel: An Old Dog Learns New Tricks

This case was prepared and written by Professors John J. Newbold, Sanjay S. Mehta, and Irfan Ahmed, Sam Houston State University, Texas. Reprinted by permission.

INTRODUCTION

Dogwood Kennel (DK) is a family-owned business offering canine boarding, training, and grooming services in Dogville, Texas. The owners of DK are Scott and Stephanie Sanderson. Stephanie's experience in the breeding, training, grooming, and boarding of dogs is complemented by Scott's 15-year background as a narcotic detection K9 sergeant.

Competitive Environment

Of the three kennels that currently operate in the county, DK is the only one that offers a full complement of services (including boarding, grooming, and training). DK is also the largest of the three in terms of number of individual kennel facilities, as well as being the lowest-priced facility in the county.

In contrast to DK's generally broad appeal, Gazebo Kennel targets dog owners through its location nearby a major regional shopping center and its focus as a child-friendly kennel. DK's other competitor, Pride Kennel, is more upscale and focuses on the boarding and training of hunting dogs. See Table 1 for a brief overview of DK and its key competitors.

Table 1
Overview of Dogwood Kennels and Key Competitors

Kennel	Number of Runs	Price (per 24 hours)	Amenities
Dogwood Kennel	40	$9.00 starting rate	Indoor and outdoor kennels; 4 ft. x 12 ft. runs; climate controlled; grooming and training facilities
Gazebo Kennel	30	$12.00 flat rate	Indoor and outdoor kennels; 4 ft. x 10 ft. runs; climate controlled; grooming facilities
Pride Kennel	12	$18.00 minimum (varies based on size of dog)	Indoor and outdoor kennels; 4 ft. x 10 ft. runs; climate controlled; training facilities

MARKETING STRATEGY FOR DOGWOOD KENNEL

Target Market and Marketing Research

Both Scott and Stephanie grew up in Dogville, Texas, and feel that they 'understand' who the dog owners are and what features and services they desire in a kennel. Prior to the introduction of a Web site and the use of data base marketing, little information was collected regarding the owners and their pets (i.e., most information was recorded by hand in a notebook). There was also no conscious attempt to segment the market.

Product/Services Strategy

DK is the only full-service kennel in the market area, offering services in all three key areas: boarding, grooming, and training. It also offers value-added services such as free baths when customers board their pets.

Price Strategy

Scott and Stephanie constantly monitor DK's competitors' price levels and consistently price their services at or slightly below their competitors for similar services. In an effort to entice customers to order more than one service at a time, they also offer "bundled" pricing for combinations of services. For example, if a customer agreed to have his or her pet groomed while it was being boarded, the customer would receive a discount from the usual price for grooming.

Promotion Strategy

Until recently, DK relied mostly on word-of-mouth communication and referrals for its business. Less than $500 is spent on a local Yellow Pages listing. In addition, DK has a black-and-white brochure that is given to customers as a reminder of the additional services offered.

Location Strategy

DK is located in an undeveloped area of Dogwood along a major interstate highway. This location reduces any noise issues associated with a kennel. The location also is very convenient for patrons who are on their way into or out of town since it is close to Dogwood's regional airport.

THE WEB SITE

The Web site also includes a "shrink-wrap" data base marketing solution that was developed specifically for kennel owner/operators.

When Scott Sanderson created the Web site for DK in 2003, his primary motivation was to learn about the Internet and post some pictures of the kennel on the Internet for friends and family to enjoy. Since then, the Web site has evolved into a useful marketing tool that includes:

- Visuals: These include photos of DK's facilities that highlight its spacious accommodations, as well as photos of Scott and Stephanie caring for their "guests."
- Maps: Maps of the location make it easy for new customers to find DK. Since the Web site was established, DK has seen its trade area expanded beyond its home county to a fringe area as far as 35 miles away. Many of these customers are attracted to DK's location near Dogwood's regional airport.
- A section on new services and suggested price bundles. This attracts customers to add extra services such as grooming. In general, DK finds that customers are now much more knowledgeable about what services it offers and tend to make use of more services per visit.
- Reservations: The Web site enables customers to make reservations for their pets online. This frees up limited management time from taking reservations via telephone and enables customers to make reservations on a 24/7 basis.

The Impact of the Data Base Marketing Tool

Recently, DK implemented a data base management software package that:
- Maintains a profile of customer preferences.
- Provides a scheduling tool for reservations.
- Assists in preparing invoices and tracking finances.

DK has begun to leverage the benefits of its customer profile and activity data through implementing a newsletter, customer surveys, a referral program, and a customer loyalty program:

- **Newsletter:** DK's newsletter is E-mailed or sent via regular mail to all of its customers. The newsletter has been a very effective platform (along with the Web site) to inform customers of new services and suggest bundled offerings.

- **Customer Surveys:** DK now undertakes customer satisfaction surveys to determine the level of customer satisfaction with its services, as well as to solicit ideas for improving its services. Based upon responses to these surveys, DK now stocks specialty dog toys and food items not available in local stores. It also offers a new pick-up/drop-off service for customers who do not have easy access to transportation and/or are physically challenged.

- **Referral Program:** DK has instituted a referral program. Customers referring a friend or relative to DK will receive credit for one free night's stay at the kennel.

-

- **Customer Loyalty Program:** DK has established a schedule of rewards based upon the frequency of use of the services. The rewards span the gamut of their services: boarding, grooming, and training. This loyalty program has proven to be an effective means of building customer relationships.

- **Customer Analysis:** Scott and Stephanie have used the data base to identify nearby areas with low market penetration. Due to customer analysis and targeted offerings, DK now attracts a large number of customers who live in retirement communities.

Questions:

1. Recommend some Internet marketing strategies that DK could develop and use to improve its market share.

2. Develop a survey that DK could use to determine the kinds of services the senior market would prefer.

3. Create a marketing plan that the Sandersons could use to market DK's services to the senior market.

4. Generate a vertical retail audit to assess DK's pricing strategy.

CASE 12

Frozen Yogurt Delight: Dealing with Service Failure and Recovery

This case was prepared and written by Professor Michael Luthy, Bellarmine University. Select names, titles, website addresses, and other identifying information have been disguised. Reprinted by permission.

INITIAL LETTER

222 West 30th Street
New York, NY 10016
April 1, 2009

Mr. Charles M. Rosen
Franchiser Director, Frozen Yogurt Delight
1010 Sunrise Boulevard
Los Angeles, CA 90045

Dear Mr. Rosen:

I am writing to relate my experience with one of your franchises. Sadly, it is not a happy one.

In late summer of last year, I purchased a frozen yogurt in your downtown New York location (555 West 4th Street). Unfortunately, the strawberry topping that I had ordered was not fresh. While the store employee, Valerie, was polite, she insisted that the strawberries were delivered that day. Based on their appearance, I was pretty sure that the strawberries were prepared the day before. Valerie offered to replace the strawberry topping with another flavor, but the other toppings looked just as bad. Instead of having an argument, I simply purchased the yogurt, had a few tastes, and then threw most of it in the garbage.

When I got home, I reported the incident on your Web site. I detailed what happened, including the store address, the date, and Valerie's name. Although my original expectations were not particularly high, I thought that I would have at have received an apology and a coupon for another yogurt. Other than the automated E-mail message acknowledging my communication, I have not received any response. After several weeks, I decided to try again. I went back to your Web site and again informed your company of my experience—as well as my frustration about not hearing back.

Sincerely,

Jack Custer

INITIAL E-MAIL RESPONSE

<u>JCUSTER@ATT.NET</u>
The acknowledgement to that message is reprinted below:

From: Fycustomersupport@trackorder.com
To: JCUSTER@ATT.NET
Subject: Arizona Pizza Pantry Incident Report #:114810
April 5, 2009

Dear Jack Custer,

Thank you for your comments. We have forwarded your feedback to our Regional Franchising Director who will work with the Store Management Team to respond to your feedback. They will contact you for further information, if necessary.

Sincerely,

Customer Service
Frozen Yogurt
<u>http://www.FY.com</u>

P.S. Please retain your Case Number in the subject line. This will help us locate your information should you need us again. This E-mail address is not set up to accept messages. Please direct any further communication through the FY Comments Website at http://www.FY.com or call us at 1-55-WE-DO-CARE.

SECOND COMPLAINT LETTER

222 West 30th Street
New York, NY 10016
May 15, 2009

Mr. Charles M. Rosen
Franchise Director, Frozen Yogurt Deight
1010 Sunrise Boulevard
Los Angeles, CA 90045

Dear Mr. Rosen:

After several additional weeks with no contact, I decided to call your "WE-DO-CARE" customer service number. I related what had by that time become a somewhat lengthy story to Joe S., a customer service person. He took down the information, as well as the incident number listed in my E-mail and then asked if I would like a person to contact me. I noted that I wanted to talk to a supervisor.

As of today (some 4 months later), I have not been contacted by anyone from your organization, at any level, locally or regionally. I am a marketing consultant by training, and I'll give you this one for free – your customer service function is broken.

Sincerely,

Jack Custer
jcuster@belsouth.net
502-555-1212

cc: Ms. Sally Cleveland, Senior Vice President of Marketing and Public Relations
cc: Mr. Ronald S. Seed, Co-Chairman of the Board of Directors, Co-President and Co-CEO

SECOND E-MAIL RESPONSE

May 20, 2009

Dear Mr. Custer,

We would like to thank you for taking the time to contact us regarding your concerns. We are very sorry to hear that you had a bad experience at a local franchise. We know you have many ice cream and yogurt brands to choose from and we appreciated that you chose to patronize FROZEN YOGURT DELIGHT.

We will be sure to pass this information to our local franchises so that a similar situation will not occur in the future. Please accept our sincere apologies for the customer service you received following your complaint.

We work hard to maintain the highest standards of product quality and customer service. It is very disappointing to hear we did not meet your expectations. Please be assured we have forwarded your comments onto our Customer Service Director, who will be sure to address these issues immediately.

Guest feedback is vital to our success and we thank you for bringing these issues to our attention. We have enclosed complimentary "Frozen Yogurt Delight Dough" ($15 in coupons for use at any of our franchises) in hopes that you will visit us again and give us the opportunity to demonstrate the excellent quality of our products.

Sincerely,

Shawna Huff
Customer Relations Director
Frozen Yogurt Delight

Questions:

1. How would you characterize the tone and content of the letter and E-mail messages written by the consumer? What was he asking for? Was it reasonable? Explain your answers.

2. Analyze Frozen Yogurt Delight's responses to the consumer complaint.

3. How can Frozen Yogurt Delight ensure that similar problems will not emerge? Your answer needs to reflect its use of franchising.

4. How would your answer to Question 2 vary if Frozen Yogurt Delight operated company-owned stores?

CASE 13

Forman Mills: From Flea Markets to Millions

This case was prepared and written by Professor Carol Kaufman-Scarborough, Rutgers University, Camden, New Jersey. Reprinted by permission.

Rick Forman took his business concept from selling T-shirts at flea markets and turned it into a $150-million retail operation (www.formanmills.com) in less than 20 years. How? By selling high-quality, name-brand products at deeply discounted prices, in stores located in urban neighborhoods.

Originally, Rick Forman sold T-shirts, sportswear, and sweatshirts to working-class customers in flea markets in Philadelphia. Forman's deeply discounted prices and devotion to the inner-city customer enabled him to grow his business quickly and profitably. Beginning with one warehouse store in 1981, Forman soon opened his first Forman Mills Clothing Factory Warehouse superstore in 1985. This signature format introduced the Forman Mills "big box" concept in a 16,000-square-foot former warehouse space in South Philadelphia. The chain now has 25 stores in seven markets (Philadelphia, Northern New Jersey, Southern New Jersey, Delaware, Maryland, New York, and Michigan).

FORMAN MILLS' OVERALL RETAIL STRATEGY

Rick Forman had a talent for identifying popular brands and optimizing value to consumers through his skills as an effective negotiator and through alliances within major manufacturers. According to Forman, "We go to the factories, overseas, we go anywhere and anyplace we can get a deal." "We're a true outlet for branded products. We overwhelm them [the customers] with the quantities. If we can get them in the door, there are very few people that will not buy." Forman Mills' warehouse operations boasts a 12-hour turnaround; this means that clothing can be bought at deep discount and onto Forman's shelves within a 12-hour period. Overhead is reduced and stores are always full of fresh merchandise, thanks to its well-managed logistics system.

Forman Mills' overall retail strategy is based on its merchandise selection, its use of urban locations, its promotional strategy, and its community service.

Merchandise Selection

Forman Mills' merchandise selection consists of of tennis-style dresses featuring National Basketball Association logos, '60s and '70s Milwaukee Brewers and San Diego Padres baseball caps, rows of oversized white T-shirts, and hundreds of pairs of blue jeans. There are school uniforms for $7.99 and long-sleeve Ravens shirts for $12.99, with brands such as Rocawear, South Pole, Ecko, Timberland, Sean John, South Pole, Baby Phat, Nike, JLo, and many others. While these are brands that customers would find in most department stores, Forman sells them at savings of up to 85 percent off suggested retail prices.

Forman Mills promotes itself as the leading retailer of "city-wear" in its market areas. Its Web site describes its assortment:

Look at all the stuff we sell:
- Sweats in 50 different styles and colors
- Designer denim
- Official team clothing
- The world's finest activewear
- Famous maker sweaters
- Designer dresses
- Name brand outerwear and footwear
- Flannels, designer leathers
- Underwear, socks, hats, T-shirts
- Knit, woven, corduroy, and velour tops, turtlenecks; mocknecks; leggings
- Warm-up suits and much more!

Underserved Locations: Bringing Life Back into Declining Neighborhoods

Forman Mills' stores are typically located in urban neighborhoods, adjacent to or directly within major cities such as Philadelphia, Baltimore, and Washington. The neighborhoods are often overlooked by retail developers since there may be few existing or successful stores. Despite the difficult task of rebuilding a once thriving retail area, Forman often establishes a solid retail base in an underserved community, creating jobs and attracting other retailers to the area.

To keep costs low, the chain uses "second-use locations" which were vacated by other merchants. The stores are all 40,000 to 125,000 square feet in size. Rather than renovating the store interior or exterior, Forman uses everything in the spaces, including store and lighting fixtures, and even shopping carts. For example, shopping carts from Ames, a failed retailer, have been refitted with Forman Mills' decals.

The chain has an extensive plan for growth over the next decade. Potential new markets include Detroit, Chicago, and Cleveland.

Promotion and Spirit

Forman Mills' stores and promotions are not conservative, dingy, or dull. Forman's trademark colors are bold yellow and red, which are used throughout its print ads, Web site, and on its storefronts. The bright yellow and red are deliberately eye-catching, designed to make the stores stand out among neighboring stores.

Its commercials make use of Forman's unique brand of catchy phrases – often annoying yet memorable. Customers are invited to "stretch those bills . . . at Forman Mills." Creative text is also often used to generate consumer excitement. The Forman Mills Web site also uses attention-getting text, such as "killer prices," "kids' summer fashion frenzy!" and "junior designer Capri blowout!"

Serving the Community

Rick Forman's community consciousness goes beyond the low prices offered to consumers. Recently, Forman Mills and its school uniform supplier donated nearly $40,000 worth of school uniform vouchers to a Philadelphia middle school in an attempt to help lower the often considerable back-to-school expenses faced by parents. The vouchers allowed students to be able to purchase up to two complete uniforms.

Similarly, Forman Mills often plays a prominent role in underwriting the expenses of local community events. For example, the fifth annual Reverend Dr. Martin Luther King, Jr. Birthday Celebration Parade in Baltimore, Maryland, was co-sponsored by Forman Mills, together with several other organizations.

Questions:

1. Describe Forman Mills' target market. Could Forman Mills use its success to move out of its current markets and expand to the mass market? Explain your answer.

2. The case states that potential markets include Detroit, Chicago, and Cleveland. How can management use census data to identify and analyze new potential markets?

3. Forman has gone beyond its original merchandise mix to include many new products and brands. Analyze them in terms of depth and width of assortment.

4. Consider the diagram of retail strategy introduced at the beginning of the text. Do you think that Forman Mills consistently follows its intended strategy? Why or why not?

CASE 14

Geographic Information Systems in Retailing

This case was prepared and written by Professors Mark R. Leipnik and Sanjay S. Mehta, Sam Houston State University, Huntsville, Texas. Reprinted by permission.

Starbucks wants to make sure its new stores achieve satisfactory sales goals, Burger King wants to ensure that cannibalization of existing units by its new units is minimal, The Gap wants to better understand the demographic characteristics in each store's trading area, Shell wants to locate new company-owned and franchised gas stations on profitable stretches of road, Kmart wants to determine which units to close to regain profitability, and Chase Manhattan Bank wants to close the now redundant branches created by a merger. These and other firms with retail operations are turning to geographic information systems (GIS) to address these and other issues. Numerous marketing consultants, location and logistics experts, and even small and medium-sized business owners and employees are now using GIS to perform spatial analysis related to retailing. Let's look at the characteristics of this emerging technology and see how it can assist retailers.

GIS CHARACTERISTICS

GIS is a specialized computer program that combines digital maps with associated descriptive attribute data. It then analyzes this data with powerful spatial analysis and mapping tools. The digital maps are stored in a special topological format in a series of layers, all of which share a common coordinate system and projection (a method for rendering in two dimensions, features that exist on the curved surface of the earth). The descriptive attribute data are stored in rows and columns as in typical data base tables, except that each record is linked to a corresponding geographic feature (such as a retail unit point location, a line representing a street segment, or a polygon representing a census tract area).

Numerous layers of data can be maintained and accessed in a GIS. For example, a layer of demographic data can be overlaid on a layer of streets and a layer of ZIP code boundaries can then be superimposed upon these two existing layers. The layers can be selectively combined. For instance, the census blocks that are contained within each of perhaps thousands of ZIP codes in a customer data base could be identified and attributes such as income, age, gender, or residential living information could be extracted. This form of analysis is referred to as polygon overlay (see figure on the left on the following page).

The polygon overlay is only one of many types of spatial analysis possible with GIS. For example, a retail analyst can generate buffer zones (these are specialized polygonal regions a specified distance from a point, line, or area). All customers located within one mile of a store location, 10 miles of an interstate highway, or 25 miles of the outer boundary of a Metropolitan Statistical Area (MSA) can be readily determined. The figure on the right of the following page shows buffer zones for a Steak & Ale restaurant in Conroe, Texas. Customer locations are symbolized by points. This figure uses streets and city boundary data from the U.S. Census Bureau's TIGER data set. In the map legend, "Str" refers to "Streets" and "Pl" refers to "Places" in data for County 339 (Montgomery County) in State 48 (Texas). More sophisticated forms of spatial analysis such as travel time analysis are also possible with specialized extensions to commercial GIS software.

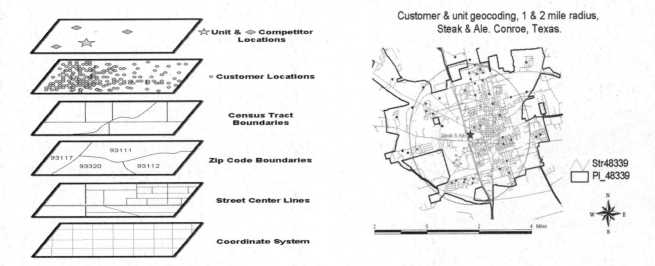

Typical Marketing Applications

Most users of GIS want to be able to see a store's locations, where their customers live, regional demographic profiles, and customer characteristics displayed on a base map. Typically, a base map is a network of streets portrayed by their centerlines, along with layers that provide boundaries for cities, counties, MSAs, and states. Also of importance are the boundaries and associated attributes of the census subdivisions including blocks, block groups, tracts, and other larger areas. The U.S. Census Bureau has created a GIS termed TIGER (Topologically Integrated Geographic Encoding and Referencing system) that contains this information (http://tiger.census.gov/). TIGER includes all of the census enumeration area boundaries, most streets, rail lines, federal and state facilities, airports, and rivers and streams, each stored as a separate layer. The demographic data linked to TIGER are updated every 10 years while the streets and infrastructure data are updated continuously and generally has a lag of about three years.

TIGER does not contain all the information a marketer might desire (e.g., location of retail units, competitor locations, and actual customer locations). These must be added to the generic GIS by geocoding. Several alternatives exist for geocoding. Many neophyte users simply "guestimate" the unit location by viewing the map and insert a point (or polygon) symbolizing the unit at that approximate location. Most commercial GIS packages have automated geocoding functions and there are services that will geocode address data for a small per-unit fee.

For the 2000 census, ZIP code tabulation areas have been created that enable marketers to reclassify census demographics into ZIP code zones. More sophisticated direct marketers are using similar approaches to determine the demographic characteristics of telephone prefix areas.

The characteristics of trading areas are a very important and useful piece of information. For example, such information can give clues as to what products a retailer should stock in multiple locations with different demographics, what promotional methods to use, and where to locate future units. The combination of trading area characteristics with actual customer locations can indicate areas where market penetration is more or less complete. An area close to a unit with apparently favorable demographic characteristics, but relatively few actual customers, may indicate an opportunity to increase sales. When this data is combined with the locations of competitor's units and spatial factors such as presence of rivers, rail lines, highways, mass transit lines, a better understanding of the trading area can be achieved.

HOW TO USE AND OBTAIN GEOSPATIAL DATA

Since GIS is a computationally intensive application, the decline in computer costs has made GIS much more affordable. At the same time, GIS software has become more user-friendly. GIS software has also become more affordable with low-end desktop mapping software from MapInfo (http://www.mapinfo.com) costing as little as $250 per copy and higher-end software such as ARCVIEW and ARCGIS from ESRI (http://www.esri.com) costing on the order of $1,000 per copy. Also, data sets such as TIGER and other data including accurate road network data, digital topographic maps, digital aerial photography, and other more specialized data sets that are now available either on CD-ROM or over the Internet, are making the previously tedious task of creating GIS data sets far easier.

GIS users frequently supplement the bare bones street centerlines of TIGER data with scanned embedded photographs of facilities such as store locations. GIS can also incorporate Computer Aided Design (CAD) drawings of floor plans and digital aerial photography or, where appropriate, satellite remotely-sensed imagery. These images can give users a big-picture feel for a given location and help to fill in the empty space between the street centerline-based representations of communities common in GIS data sets like TIGER.

Future Prospects
The Web-based GIS area has continued to grow, as the leading GIS software vendors (ESRI, MapInfo, and Intergraph) have all rolled out Internet-based mapping and spatial analysis products that allow huge geospatial data bases to be stored on a central server and be accessed with conventional browsers. In the near future, GIS users will be able to access a wider range of geodemographic data over the Internet, obtain re-segmented data like the PRIZM data set from vendors such as Claritas (http://www.claritas.com/), or Geolytics (http://www.censuscd.com/), and create customized printable maps, charts, and reports all using Web-based solutions.

GIS is also moving from the server and desktop computer to the vehicle and field-based laptop and is starting to migrate to mobile console and hand-held PDA and palm devices, many of which will also be outfitted with GPS and wireless Internet capabilities.

Questions:

1.   Go to the TIGER Web site (http://tiger.census.gov) and use the interactive mapping feature of the TIGER Map Server (TMS) to generate a map of streets and other features. Then use the census statistics data to create color coded maps of income, race, or other demographic characteristics at the census block group level for your hometown or the city or town in which you presently reside.

2.   Since TIGER demographic data is frequently 10 or more years out of date, what kinds of mistakes in retail site location can be made as a result of using old TIGER data? Name five.

3. How might a major retailer like Radio Shack, The Gap, or Toys "R" Us, which gathers customer ZIP code and telephone information, create a GIS with this information?

4. What other types (layers) of information might be relevant to retailers besides streets, unit location, and customer locations?

5. Is a circular buffer zone generated around a unit location the best way to estimate a trade area? What factors besides straight-line distance from a potential customer to a store might determine shopping behavior and frequency? How many of these factors could be mapped and analyzed using a GIS? Explain your answers.

CASE 15

The Golden Fleece

This case was prepared and written by Professor Doreen Burdalski, Albright College. Reprinted by permission.

Lucky Stores is a discount store chain located in the Northeast region of the United States. It currently has 25 stores located in Pennsylvania, New Jersey, and Delaware. Lucky's assortment includes hardlines and softlines merchandise. National brands like Hanes, Carter's, Hoover, Westbend, and Fieldcrest are an important part of its merchandise mix. Forty percent of its mix is national name brands. Approximately 25 percent of its merchandise is private label. Lucky's competitors include Kmart and Wal-Mart. Lucky has been in the Philadelphia area for over 30 years. It was established for 25 years before Wal-Mart came into the area. The chain prides itself on the cleanliness of its stores. It considers itself a "step above" the national discounters in terms of quality and presentation of merchandise.

Ima Spender is the junior sportswear buyer for Lucky Stores. She is responsible for purchasing junior pants, tops, and coordinates for the chain. This merchandise is targeted toward pre-teen and teenage girls. The sizes run small/medium/large and from size 3 to 13. Her department does about $10 million a year in sales and the gross margin is 45 percent.

Late last November, Spender received a phone call from a jobber who offered her 9,000 dozen basic fleece pants at a cost of $2.00 each. This merchandise became available because a regional sporting goods chain in the Northwest went out of business and could not commit to the order. Spender's sales were sluggish at the time and she was overbought; but she recognized what a great deal was being offered to her. These fleece pants normally retail for $7.99. Spender went to her divisional merchandise manager with the deal. Together, they contacted the store managers to get their feedback. The managers were excited about the purchase and promised to merchandise the fleece pants on promotional tables throughout the main aisle of their stores. Ima Spender purchased the fleece pants and retailed them for $5.00 each. They came packed in cartons of five dozen. The colors and sizes were assorted. There were men's and women's sizes mixed together in the cartons.

The stores complained about the mix of sizes and colors, particularly the gold color. They also complained about the amount of manpower it took to keep the promotional tables straightened up and neat looking; but by January, the stores had sold out and were getting customer requests for more fleece pants. Customers wrote letters to the president of Lucky Stores telling how much they liked the $5.00 fleece pants.

Ima Spender increased the sales in her department that year by $500,000 over the previous year. She sold $520,000 worth of $5.00 fleece pants. She needed $20,000 in markdowns on the fleece pants to sell out her inventory. These sales actually made the difference in the ready-to-wear division, making its sales plan for the year. Spender's divisional merchandise manager attributed the success of the season to the $5.00 fleece pants sales. The president of the company was very pleased with the happy customers; however, the store managers complained about being left with promotional tables filled with gold fleece pants in January that needed to be marked down to $2.00 retail.

It is now March and Ima Spender is in the process of developing a six-month forecast and budget for the coming fall that will include August through January. Upper management is looking for a 3 percent sales increase over last fall and a 10 percent increase in gross margin percent. Spender's 5 percent increase last fall was totally attributed to the sales of the $5.00 fleece pants. The jobber that she purchased the fleece pants from cannot guarantee the merchandise will be available for sale this year. She has concerns about being able to make the same advantageous purchase this fall. In her ten years of buying experience, Spender has never seen any department plan less sales than it did the previous year.

Questions:

1.   What important factors are determined in the forecasting and budgeting process?

2.   What must the retailer consider when forecasting sales for the upcoming season?

3.   What are Ima Spender's key concerns with forecasting and budgeting sales for this fall?

4.   Should Spender plan the 3 percent sales increase that upper management is asking for this fall? Explain your answer.

CASE 16

Hayfield House Museum Store

This case was prepared and written by Professor Sandra Mottner, Western Washington University, Bellingham, Washington. Reprinted by permission.

Hayfield House is a historic house and farm in the Pacific Northwest, about a half-hour from Seattle, Washington. Hayfield House operates as a museum that highlights early homesteading in an area that once was the Oregon Territory.

The historic farmhouse and accompanying acreage are owned and managed by the Hayfield Trust, a nonprofit organization. The trust's primary mission is to educate the public about early settlement and farming in the Pacific Northwest. Of special interest is the role of the Native American and Asian community in the role of settling and developing the area. The museum also maintains and preserves a collection of buildings, heritage breeds of farm animals, period-specific plants, and antique farm implements.

Hayfield House has experienced rapid growth in its visitor population due to the outstanding efforts of its relatively new museum director. Data on annual visits are shown in Table 1.

Table 1: Hayfield House Historical Visitation

VISITATION	2004	2005	2006
Adults	100,000	125,000	145,000
Tour group members	0	10,000	20,000
Senior citizens (65+)	20,000	22,000	23,500
Children (5-12)*	20,000	37,500	65,000
TOTAL	140,000	194,500	253,500

* Children under 5 years of age are free and not counted in the visitation numbers.

While the number of paid visitors has grown significantly, the museum's endowment is relatively limited. The admission fees and profits from its gift shop sales contribute only a partial portion of the museum's total operating expenses. A new membership program has recently begun to build a stronger membership base. Through the membership program, museum members receive free annual admission to Hayfield House plus a 10 percent discount at the gift shop in exchange for an annual membership fee.

Hayfield House's gift shop is currently located in the entrance hall of the house. Its sales are limited to a few books and postcards that are sold at the ticket counter. Recently, the museum director and the board of the Hayfield Trust have decided to hire a full-time museum store manager and to dedicate 1,200 square feet in an old storage building to a gift shop. The new gift shop will also have a ticket counter that should use no more than 200 square feet of the space. In this layout arrangement, visitors to Hayfield House will have to pass through the store to purchase their admission tickets, as well as to the parking lot (after completion of the house tour). The museum director hopes that the gift shop's location near the entrance and exit of the museum has a significant positive effect on gift shop sales.

The new museum store manager is charged with several tasks. These include: (1) determining an initial financial investment for the merchandise inventory in the gift shop store, (2) allocating the inventory investment among multiple product categories, and (3) developing a list of key items for the store. The store manager is a member of the Museum Stores Association (www.museumdistrict.com) and regularly attends its annual conference. Consequently, the museum store manager is familiar with the issue of the Internal Revenue Service's related-use ruling. This ruling states that sales by a nonprofit store must be related to the nonprofit organization's primary mission. Anything sold at the museum shop that is not related to its mission is subject to taxation and could potentially endanger the organization's nonprofit status. As a result of this ruling, the gift shop's merchandise should educate the buyer about site-related history.

Tables 2 and 3 contain data on some comparable museum stores. The museum store manager went to each of the sites and has made some notes about each one. Here are the notes:

Table 2: Museum Store Comparative Annual Data

	McGregor's Farm	The Old Manse	Villa del Farm
Museum store net sales	$765,000	$112,500	$2,098,750
Store size (square feet)	3,000	250	1,250
Inventory turnover	5.5 times	1.1 times	2.75 times
Gross margin %	40%	49%	45%
Sales by category:			
Books and publications	$229,500	$55,000	$835,000
Souvenirs (postcards, etc.)	$ 5,000	$ 1,000	$ 22,500
Clothing (T-shirts, etc.)	$ 95,000	0	$110,000
Food	$150,000	0	$206,250
Jewelry	$ 10,000	$15,000	$195,000
Toys	$200,000	0	$120,000
Plants	0	0	$250,000
Other gifts	$ 75,500	$41,500	$360,000

Table 3: Museum Visitation Comparative Annual Data

	McGregor's Farm	The Old Manse	Villa del Farm
Adults	204,000	35,000	237,250
Tour group members	102,000	0	36,500
Senior citizens (65+)	25,500	12,500	54,750
Children (5-12)*	178,500	2,500	36,500
TOTAL	510,000	50,000	365,000

* Children under 5 years of age are free and not counted in the visitation numbers.

McGregor's Farm

This is a farm museum near Sacramento, California. The original owners of the farm were a family who settled in the area during the California Gold Rush. The farm features on-site livestock, which includes plow horses, chickens, cows, and hogs, as well as pony rides. The gift shop sells books about the gold rush and early California history, as well as a huge variety of jams and jellies–all with the McGregor label on them. A lot of stuffed animals are also available, mostly farm animals. The farm museum also sells coloring books related to farming.

The Old Manse

A Victorian period home, this museum/historic site is located in Portland, Oregon, and is significant because it was a parsonage for an early frontier church. The volunteer staff dress in period costumes as they escort visitors through the house and talk about life in Oregon in the middle and late 1800s. The yard of the house is filled with vintage roses that were planted by the first inhabitants of the house. The small shop area sells mostly books on Oregon history, roses, and flower gardening. It also sells postcards and a small assortment of Victorian-styled jewelry.

Villa del Farm

This museum site is located outside of Los Angeles and includes an old and very large building that originally housed a Spanish mission. The mission was turned into a lavish residence in the 1800s. Many embellishments were later on added to the house and grounds by a wealthy early film star. The wealthy landowners who converted the mission to a residence had an olive orchard, remnants of which still exist today. Pools and fountains put in by the film star still work and dot the landscaped area around the house. The store is in the area that once was a horse stable. Aside from books on early California missions and biographies of the film star, there is also an extensive assortment of gifts related to olives. There are olive-shaped dishes, olive oil, olive oil-based soaps, and recipe books that use olives and olive oils.

Questions:

1. Interpret the data in Tables 1, 2, and 3. Based on the historical trend (Table 1), estimate visitation for Hayfield House for 2007.

2. Estimate the net sales for the Hayfield House gift shop for 2007 in its new expanded location. Explain your estimate.

3. The board members of Hayfield House will allow you to spend 20 percent more than your estimated average stock on hand to open the store. How many dollars will you allocate to each of the categories shown in Table 2? Explain your reasoning.

4. Suggest a product for each of the merchandise categories in Table 2 that could be developed specifically for Hayfield House and meets the "related use" criteria.

CASE 17

Island Grill Restaurant, Jamaica

This case was prepared and written by Professor Jonathan N. Goodrich, Florida International University. Reprinted by permission.

INTRODUCTION

In November 1991, a small group of Jamaicans opened a restaurant in Kingston, Jamaica, called Chicken Supreme. The restaurant grilled chicken using oregano and parsley. While a number of well-known international fast food chains such as KFC and Burger King had outlets in Jamaica, the taste of the food sold by these firms was not readily accepted by the Jamaican consumer. On the whole, Jamaicans prefer and are used to eating foods such as chicken, fish, and rice and peas, not hamburgers. While there are small restaurants in the market that offer jerk chicken, Island Grill is the only established local franchise chain that offers jerk chicken. The name of the restaurant was changed to Island Grill in 1998 to reflect its sale of local foods.

The Island Grill chain has grown to ten outlets on the island. The main products offered are jerk chicken, BBQ chicken, fried plantains, and other regional specialties. The chain has five locations in Kingston, one in Spanish Town, two in Ocho Rios, and two in Montego Bay. The two most profitable restaurants are at the international airports in Kingston and Montego Bay. All of the chain's restaurants are located in high-traffic areas such as LOJ Plaza in Spanish Town, Sovereign Plaza in Kingston, the Donald Sangster International Airport in Montego Bay, and the Norman Manley International Airport in Kingston.

In April 2001, the company opened its first U.S. restaurant in Lauderdale Lakes, Fort Lauderdale, about 50 miles north of Miami, Florida. In May 2002, a second store was opened in Pembroke Pines, about 40 miles north of Miami, Florida. In December 2002, both restaurants were closed due to inadequate sales, poor location planning, and lack of cultural awareness. For example, one of its restaurants had a high traffic count at lunch; however, many Jamaicans prefer to eat out in the evenings. At the time of the closings, Island Grill employed 70 permanent and temporary workers at these two U.S. restaurants.

The Island Grill chain reported sales revenues close to U.S. $10 million annually (each Island Grill restaurant has sales revenue of about U.S. $1 million annually), and the chain has 419 employees.

Retail Strategy

While the restaurant's major target market is Jamaicans, its secondary market consists of tourists visiting Jamaica while on vacation. As a result, the chain's restaurants at the island's two major airports (Kingston and Montego Bay) are among its most profitable.

The restaurant's signature dish is Jamaican jerk chicken, grilled over an open flame in Island Grill's own jerk sauce (a combination of allspice, scallion, thyme, and scotch bonnet pepper). Other popular products are jerk fish and the special jerk hamburger. Each of these main courses is complemented by pumpkin rice, coconut callaloo rice, soup, green banana fries, rice and peas, white rice, fried plantains, and festival (a fritter made from cornmeal). Drinks served include bottled water, soft drinks, carrot juice, orange juice, pineapple juice, lemonade, and Irish Moss (made from a type of seaweed, rum, condensed milk, sugar, and cinnamon). Ice cream, cake, cookies, and sweet potato pudding are also served.

Table 1 compares some of Island Grill's local prices with that of KFC, the leading chicken fast-food chain, and Burger King, the leading hamburger giant on the island. This table demonstrates Island Grill's competitive pricing strategy which was to provide a product at a price that was viewed as value for money. Prices are in Jamaican dollars. Currently (2005), U.S. $1 = Jamaican $60. See Table 1.

Island Grill heavily advertised and promoted in both the print and electronic media in Jamaica. The restaurant chain frequently has print ads in Jamaica's three newspapers (the *Gleaner*, *Herald*, and *Observer*). It also places ads on Jamaican radio stations and JBC (the Jamaica Broadcasting Corporation), which is the island's major television station. About $100,000 per year (10 percent of yearly sales) per outlet is spent on advertising. The chain's promotion slogan is currently "Real Food, Real Taste, Real Good."

Island Grill has 419 employees. The management team includes Chief Executive Officer and Managing Director, Thalia Lyn; General Manager, Dennis Hawkins; Marketing Coordinator, Erica Hanson; a financial controller; a training/human resource manager; an operations manager; a special projects manager; and a maintenance manager. Howard Mitchell, who is an attorney, serves as Board Chairman. Figure 1 shows the organizational structure of the company.

Table 1
Price Comparison

Island Grill	Price	KFC	Price	Burger King	Price
Jus' Nuff (1/4 chicken – Jerk or BBQ, festival, and soda)	$175	**Meal Deal** (2-piece, fries, and soda)	$185	N/A	N/A
Satisfaction (1/4 chicken – Jerk or BBQ, festival, rice, and soda)	$200	**Big Deal** (3-piece, fries, and soda)	$240	N/A	N/A
Chicken Value (1/2 chicken – Jerk or BBQ, festival)	$505	**Combo** (6-piece, fries, and soda)	$500	N/A	N/A
Session Pack (whole chicken – Jerk or BBQ, rice or 8 festivals	$595	**Family Combo** (9-piece, fries, and soda)	$695	N/A	N/A
Jerk cheese burger	$120	N/A		Whopper	$210
Chicken sandwich combo	$200	**Zinger Combo**	$195	Chicken sandwich	$195

Questions:

1.   Discuss the pros and cons of Island Grill's strategies in expanding in Jamaica.

2.   Comment on the chain's lack of success in the United States.

3.   How could Island Grill have overcome its U.S. expansion difficulties?

4.   Evaluate Island Grill's organization chart.

CASE 18

Just a Joke or Sexual Harassment?

This case was prepared and written by Professor Gale Jaeger, Marywood University, Scranton, Pennsylvania. Reprinted by permission.

A successful upscale department store in Manhattan needed to hire a fur manager/buyer for its fur salon. After spending 28 years at the store, the former manager/buyer decided to retire in October, just before the major fur selling season. It would be important to have someone in place as soon as possible.

In late October, the department store's employment manager received a cover letter and resume from a candidate, John Gleason, who was related to the previous fur manager/buyer. Mr. Gleason expressed an interest in relocating to the New York area to be closer to his family. But while he always worked in the fur industry, he never held a management level position. Nevertheless, he presented himself well, seemed enthusiastic, and appeared to have a lively personality. With some reservations, but knowing that the busy season was upon them, the human resource director agreed to make a job offer to John Gleason. He began his new position the second week of November.

By early December, it appeared that a good selection had been made. The department had a very successful holiday season which exceeded planned sales and profits for the current year. The store's group vice-president contacted John to let him know how pleased he was with John's performance.

Just after the holiday rush was winding down, several problems began to emerge concerning John Gleason. Two long-term employees of the fur salon made an appointment to meet with the store's human resource director. The ladies were quite concerned over Mr. Gleason's continued telling of inappropriate jokes to them and other fellow workers. The women objected to these jokes and were embarrassed. They told the human resource director that they continually asked John Gleason to refrain from such jokes in their presence. In response, John would typically tell them that they were only little jokes to "liven things up around here."

When asked how often the joke telling occurred, the women estimated that it was once a week for the past seven weeks. Finally, they felt they had to report this behavior, which they found humiliating and demeaning. One tearfully asked that Mr. Gleason not be told who had mentioned these events for fear of reprisal.

When called into the human resource director's office, John Gleason appeared quite shocked. He

74

reiterated that his jokes were well intentioned and that many other employees welcomed his humor. He said he believed it was the two "old ladies" who must have complained because they were the only ones who could have objected in any way. He said he kept telling them they should learn to take a joke.

For the next three weeks, things were quiet; business was good and all seemed to be cleared up. However, one evening as closing time approached, there was a knock at the human resource director's door. One of the women from the fur salon entered and was angry and shaken. She said she and her co-worker had avoided Mr. Gleason for the last few weeks and everything had been better. Tonight he called her into his office to discuss her sales report. As she left the office, he told her to "loosen up."

Questions:

1.   Do you believe that Mr. Gleason's behavior constituted sexual harassment? Why or why not?

2.   Does the human resource director bear any of the responsibility for this unfortunate circumstance? Why or why not?

3.   What should the next step be in this situation?

4.   What actions should the human resource director take to eliminate or minimize such situations in the future?

CASE 19

Large Retailer Demands Alienate Small Manufacturers

This case was prepared and written by Professor Suzanne G. Marshall, California State University, Long Beach. Reprinted by permission.

The ability of manufacturers and retailers to negotiate the terms under which they conduct business has eroded over the past two decades due to the power of the retailer increasing and the power of the supplier decreasing. Vera Campbell, President of Design Zone, a manufacturer of misses' and junior knit wear with sales of $15 million annually, and Susan Crank, CEO of Lunada Bay, a women's swimwear and activewear licensee for Mossimo and others, with sales of $60 million annually, speak of the power shift in the apparel industry and its negative impact on small manufacturers.

Prior to the 1980s, apparel manufacturers held a high degree of channel power due to the fact that the demand for their products exceeded the supply. This is described as a "push" system— whereas whatever goods are produced are pushed through the system to buyers who had limited choice options. In the 1980s, department stores began to merge together into large ownership groups such as Federated Department Stores (Macy's, Bloomingdale's, Rich's, Sterns, Goldsmiths, Burdines, and Jordan Marsh). As a result, buying became more centralized. Buyers bought in large quantities to supply inventory for large groups of stores all over the country rather than for a small chain in one city. Simultaneously, apparel manufacturing companies grew at a rapid pace which increased competition. As a result of the merge of retailers into fewer but more powerful conglomerates, and the increased competition among a larger number of apparel manufacturers, channel power shifted to those retailers with the "big pencils."

Realizing their higher elevation on the power channel, retailers began to shift some of the responsibilities that have traditionally been that of the retailer to the manufacturer. Manufacturers, especially smaller ones, felt that they had little power to negotiate, knowing if they refused to comply with large retailers' demands, there were plenty of other manufacturers who would supply the larger retailers. Crank and Campbell cite several examples of demands by retailers that cut into manufacturers' already narrow profit margins:

- Chargebacks—Each of the major retail ownership groups write a routing guide which sets forth rules of shipping to which the manufacturer must strictly comply. The rules cover areas such as where to attach the address label, whether the invoice goes inside or on the outside of the box, and whether shipments should be consolidated or broken down and sent to individual stores. Each notebook of rules is complex in its details and each retailer has its own notebook of rules. "I'd have to hire MBAs to work in my warehouse to understand this," complained Crank, knowing if she did not strictly comply, she would be levied a heavy "chargeback" fee (a deduction from the invoiced amount) from the retailer for having to correct the problem.

- Merchandise Preparation—Manufacturers are now responsible for tagging merchandise that involves not only price tagging, but also care labels and promotion-related tagging (which indicates the maker of certain fibers such as Dupont's Lycra). Crank was pressed to purchase both a hanging rack system and a bagging system for her warehouse, costing thousands of dollars, so that she could ship her swimwear on hangers and in bags making them "floor ready."

- Merchandisers and Specialists—Manufacturers (such as Quiksilver, St. John, and Liz Claiborne) now hire merchandisers whose main job is to visit the manufacturer's retail accounts and insure their product is being given visibility and is visually appealing. Merchandisers also work with the receiving department to insure the goods are placed on the floor in a timely manner. Similarly, many manufacturers hire retail specialists and place them in their key retail doors to sell only that manufacturer's merchandise.

- Profit Cutting Demands—There are several common retail practices that cut into the potential profit of their suppliers:
    1. Advancing the season—Campbell explained that retailers are breaking price (taking a markdown) on goods earlier and earlier each year, which eliminates the potential of a sell-through at the original retail price. Retailers explain that if they have a sale on January 15, 2000, they must "anniversary" that sale the next year to make their figures.
    2. Markdown guarantees—The retailer expects the manufacturer to share the loss of profit from any markdowns, regardless of how early the markdown was taken in the season.

3.   Automatic deduction for damages—Several retailers automatically deduct a percentage from the manufacturer's invoice to cover potential damages. Crank explains that she has only .3 percent damages and resents having to pay for the poor quality of her competitors.

In summary, both Campbell and Crank feel increased pressure from their retail customers. On one hand, they want to sell to the power retailers because of the larger orders, but on the other hand, they feel these retailers "own you."

Questions:

1.   Take the side of the retailer and make an argument supporting each demand.

2.   Take the side of the manufacturer and respond to the retailer.

3.   Develop a compromise strategy that might work for both sides. What would the strengths and weaknesses of your strategy be?

4.   What do you think is the future for small manufacturers? How can they remain competitive?

CASE 20

Larissa's: Assessing Competition in a Changing Retail Environment

This case was prepared and written by Professor Michelle Morganosky, University of Illinois at Urbana-Champaign. Reprinted by permission.

Larissa's is an independently owned specialty store that features gifts, collectibles, and home décor. What sets Larissa's apart from its competitors is its depth of assortment. The store's advertisements boast that Larissa's is "North America's largest gift and collectible shop." At first glance, the advertising sounds like old-fashioned puffery. However, once inside Larissa's, most shoppers concede that the advertising slogan is appropriate.

Larissa's is located in a mid-size city in the Midwest region of the United States adjacent to an old railroad line. The geographic market is typical in terms of competition with the usual mix of Hallmark specialty stores, a Pier 1 store, two department stores, and discounters such as Target, Meijer, and Wal-Mart.

Larissa's expansive building contains room after room of themed areas. The store has separate departments devoted to holiday/Christmas ornaments, bath and body products, cards and gift wrapping materials, candles, collectible dolls, and glass and crystal collectibles. While its prices are competitive, Larissa's specializes in middle to very high-end price points. Whereas there is an extensive depth of assortment, each item is stocked in limited quantities to give the impression this is indeed a "one-of-a-kind" shop. Larissa's maintains a customer data base; it is used on a very limited basis for seasonal mailings.

Professor Lee first started to shop at Larissa's over 20 years ago when it was originally a small antiques store. The two owners, who were professors of East European and Russian Studies at the nearby university, used the store as an extension of their interest in antiques and collectibles. Over time, they would add "special finds" from their travels to Eastern Europe and Russia to the store's assortment.

Professor Lee was dismayed when she heard rumors that Larissa's might be closing. Since she personally knew the owners, she rushed right over to find out what was going on. As the owners explained to Professor Lee, they were having some health problems and had difficulties hiring a suitable store manager to run the store. Professor Lee herself had been thinking about early retirement and is contemplating purchasing the store.

Questions:

1. Based on retail strategy mix (merchandise, location, prices), explain the potential advantages that Larissa's has over its competitors.

2. What suggestions do you have for the present owners to help find a suitable buyer for Larissa's?

3. What key information does Professor Lee need to obtain before making the decision to buy Larissa's?

4. Should Professor Lee buy Larissa's? Why or why not?

CASE 21

The Loan: A Case on Communication

This case was prepared and written by Professors Edward C. Brewer and Terence L. Holmes, Murray State University, Kentucky. Reprinted by permission.

Ann and Jay were excited. They had just come from viewing a house with their realtor, Ellie. The house was perfect! It was everything they had ever wanted. The three-bedroom, two-bath house was situated in a quaint neighborhood at the end of a cul-de-sac. The backyard was almost half an acre–perfect for their two dogs. Ann was expecting twins in two months, so moving from their cramped one-bedroom apartment was not only thrilling, but was a necessity. Ann and Jay had scrimped and saved for five years in preparation for the purchase of their first home. The asking price would be a stretch for their budget because Ann was taking maternity leave at the end of the month. She hoped to return to her job in eight weeks, but she knew it was possible that taking care of two babies might delay her return to work. Therefore, she and Jay were trying to keep the payments manageable on his income alone. With the down payment they had saved, they were certain they could make this work.

Ann and Jay needed to determine how much of a loan they could qualify for, so they could make an offer on the house. The asking price for the house was $179,000. With the $50,000 they had saved for the down payment, Ann and Jay had calculated that they could afford a $125,000 loan on Jay's income alone. That would allow them to make a $175,000 offer on the home, a figure the realtor had assured them would be acceptable to the seller. However, the catch was that the seller's attorney insisted that the buyers secure a written loan commitment as of Friday prior to going to contract. The attorney explained that the seller was being transferred out of the country, and wanted to be assured that the deal would go through. It was already Tuesday.

The Promise

Ann and Jay went immediately to see Robert, a loan officer at Community Bank. Robert had recently been promoted to loan officer, having been with the bank for four years. Robert was a friend of Ann's nephew and Ann and Jay had known him for six years. It was only natural that they would think of Robert when it came time to purchase a house.

Robert assured Ann and Jay that he didn't see any problem with the couple's ability to secure the commitment as of Friday. He felt the loan would be approved quickly. "It will probably be approved by Thursday, and you can have the written loan commitment as soon as your loan is approved," he assured them.

Ann and Jay drove to see their realtor to make the offer. They told Ellie that they would like to offer $175,000 on the home and that they could go to contract on Friday. Ellie said she would immediately discuss the offer with the seller and would call them that afternoon to let them know if the seller accepted their offer. That afternoon, Ellie called with the good news. The seller had accepted their offer. However, that morning, another offer had been made for the full $179,000 – on an "all cash" basis. The second offer would not require any financing. Because their offer had been made and accepted first, Ann and Jay would get the house; but if they didn't receive the written commitment from the bank as of Friday, they would lose the house and the house would sell to the family who had made the second offer. Jay and Ann assured Ellie they would be able to receive the commitment as of Friday directly after the loan was approved.

The Good News

Later that afternoon, Charlotte, another loan officer at Community Bank, was in a meeting with Robert. Charlotte had been a loan officer for several years. After the meeting, she told Robert that she overheard him talking to the couple about their loan and asked him why he told them they would be approved by Thursday and that they would have the commitment as soon as the loan was approved. Robert replied, "We are usually pretty quick; I don't see any problem." Charlotte responded, "You know as often as not, it takes 3 days to approve, and that it is always 1 to 2 business days after approval to receive the written commitment." Robert then said, "They will probably be approved by Thursday, but even if they aren't approved until Friday or Monday, they aren't likely to have a closing on the house for several weeks." "I hope you're right," Charlotte sighed.

Thursday came and Ann and Jay were getting anxious. Ann called Robert twice during the day to see if the loan had been approved. Robert assured Ann that he would call them when he knew something, but that Friday would be the latest he expected for approval.

Friday morning, Ann and Jay anxiously waited for Community Bank to open. They had both taken the day off to prepare for the closing on their new house that afternoon. The phone rang at 9:05 and Robert notified the couple that their loan was approved. Jay quickly responded, "Thank you; we will be there in 10 minutes," and immediately hung up the phone. Robert wondered why they would be coming to see him.

The Misunderstanding

Eight minutes later, Ann and Jay walked into Robert's office requesting their written commitment. Robert explained that it would be Monday or Tuesday before their written commitment would be ready. In exasperation, Ann said, "You assured us that we could have the written commitment as soon as the loan was approved." She began crying as she said, "We are supposed to go to contract on the house at 1:30 this afternoon." Agitated, Jay demanded the check. "You told us we could have the commitment as soon as we were approved and we need the written document this morning." Robert apologized and said, "When I said 'as soon as you are approved,' I meant it would be within 1 to 2 business days. I'm sure you can delay the contract until next Monday or Tuesday." "There is a contingency offer," Ann sobbed. "The other buyers have offered the seller full price and have the cash in hand!" Jay shouted.

"I'm sorry," Robert said. "The best I can do is put a rush on it and have it for you on Monday." Jay angrily tore up the application and approval and threw it on Robert's desk. Ann was weeping uncontrollably as Jay guided her through the lobby. "Monday, we will close our accounts and never return to Community Bank!" Jay screamed at Robert as they left the bank.
Charlotte scanned the bank's other customers who observed this incident, and entered Robert's office. "What was that all about?" she asked.

Questions:

1. What went wrong?

2. What could these people involved have done to prevent the misunderstanding?
   - Ann and Jay
   - Robert
   - Ellie
   - Charlotte

3. How did time play a factor in the events depicted in the case?

CASE 22

Mall Anchors Away: The Plastic Models Place

This case was prepared and written by Professor Terence L. Holmes, Murray State University, Kentucky. Reprinted by permission.

Frank Runyon started his retail business just after finishing high school in Cincinnati. Ever since he was a child, Frank enjoyed working with his father, grandfather, and uncles on various types of scale models. He had become quite skilled at customizing boxed model kits and won ribbons and other prizes in contests all over the United States. Finally, one of his uncles talked to him about making a business out of his hobby. His uncle told him, "Frank, you've got what 90 percent of retailers don't have–passion. You can do it!"

Frank started his model business selling materials, tools, and accessories with just a few thousand dollars of his own savings in addition to loans from family members. He chose a location in a small strip center in an eastern Cincinnati suburb. For more than a decade, the store thrived. People came to The Plastic Models Place for models and much more. Some customers would spend hours talking with Frank about techniques for building models. Many customers commented that Frank's store had more of what they needed than many larger stores.

By the late 1980s, business had slowed and Frank wondered how he might get his traffic pattern back into high gear. His uncle, now retired to Florida, advised him to take a marketing class at a local college. Frank enrolled in both an introductory marketing course, as well as a retail management course. Frank hosted a model-building workshop, with each participant building a display-quality finished model by the end of class. He also sponsored an annual model-building contest. Frank wrote press releases to promote the contest, used cooperative advertising funds from his suppliers, and invited local newspapers to cover the contest. These activities stimulated sales for several years, but business settled back to a slow, stable level.

His store was showing a bit of age, with its old display fixtures and lighting, worn carpeting, a cracked concrete walkway outside the front door, and a sign that was dated. However, Frank couldn't see spending several thousand dollars for store renovations. He hoped to wring a few more years out of the business and then perhaps sell out or close.

In the end, it was something new Frank learned that helped him save his business. His 12-year-old son, Bill, showed him an article about the Web and its potential impact on marketing. In 1994, Frank Runyon went back to his local college and completed a course on Internet marketing. Within three months, Frank put much of what he'd learned into practice. Finally, just after Christmas of 1996, The Plastic Model Place opened its online presence.

Frank had always done most of his business from greater Cincinnati, probably 75 percent of it according to ZIP codes of purchasers he had analyzed. The remaining 25 percent was from outside the city; these were primarily consumers who had heard good things from his customers or who had seen news items about the contest or the workshops. These people lived closer to several other hobby shops, but drove the extra distance to The Plastic Models Place due to its selection, reputation, and customer advice.

With the Web site now functioning, Frank soon realized he would have to reassess his store's overall strategy. For example, he would leave work disappointed that few Internet sales had come in, but by the next morning, perhaps a dozen such orders would be waiting. He received orders from all over the country and even a few from international customers.

The increased Web sales contributed to added profitability in other ways. The additional sales generated discounts from some suppliers. In some instances, Frank could get a customer order for a unique item and then purchase that item from a supplier after the sale. The increased sales also increased Frank's ability to use cooperative advertising allowances from his suppliers. Lastly, the Web was useful in selling closeouts and special buys.

Bill, now 21 and a college senior, was seasoned and ready to take over The Plastic Models Place. He told Frank he wanted to shift operations even further onto the Web, mentioning a couple of success stories he had studied: Model Expo (http://www.modelexpo-online.com) and Internet Hobbies (http://www.internethobbies.com).

Questions:

1. Discuss the difficulties in processing orders from outside of Cincinnati, including international orders.

2. Evaluate the promotion efforts Frank Runyon used over the years, as described in the case.

3. Describe the advantages of the Web in increasing the profitability for The Plastic Models Place.

4. Discuss how the marketing activities of The Plastic Models Place's store and Web-based sales can be better integrated.

CASE 23

The Prince of Cruises: Choosing a Store Location

This case was prepared and written by Professor Allan R. Miller, Towson State University, Maryland. Reprinted by permission.

Michael Charlotte has been a travel agent for over 15 years. For the last seven, he has worked as an outside agent specializing in cruise travel and tours, primarily for groups (such as members of senior citizen groups, fraternal organizations, and religious-based organizations). As an outside agent, Charlotte operates as an independent contractor for the travel agency, Go Somewhere Vacations. Charlotte and his agency divide the commissions on bookings he generates, generally about 10 percent of the vacation price. In contrast, an inside agent is an employee of the agency and is usually paid on the basis of a salary.

Go Somewhere Vacations is the largest travel agency in Bel Air, Maryland, which is a residential town located about 30 miles north of Baltimore. The agency is on the main street in Bel Air's central business district.

Recently, Charlotte decided he wanted to fulfill his lifelong dream of operating his own agency. He has a moderate base of clients who he feels would continue to book their vacations through him. In addition, Charlotte feels he can expand his client base. As in the past, he plans to continue specializing in cruise travel and tours. He wants to call his agency The Prince of Cruises.

Charlotte is considering three alternative types of location for his new agency: a home/office arrangement (in which the agency would be operated out of a converted garage space in his home), leasing a store site in a local Bel Air shopping center (about one-quarter mile from Go Somewhere Vacations' current location), or renting space in an office building in downtown Bel Air. Regardless of the location chosen, each alternative would require approximately a $17,500 investment for office furniture and furnishings, computer equipment and modem hookups, and telephone systems and wiring. However, each alternative has totally different characteristics in terms of its trading area and customer traffic.

By operating the agency out of his house, Charlotte would save rental expenses. The home/office arrangement would also enable him to conduct business on weekends and in the evenings, when most agencies are closed. However, the ability to attract walk-in clients would be severely limited due to the absence of signs, the lack of pedestrian traffic, and the need to comply with Bel Air's strict residential zoning regulations. The home/office setup would also require an additional $7,000 expense to properly wire, panel, and insulate Charlotte's former two-car garage. Lastly, Charlotte would have to develop an arrangement with an authorized travel agency to be able to sell airline tickets from a home office.

Although the home/office alternative would take him a longer time to develop a new client base, Charlotte's expenses would be lowest under this alternative. Charlotte projects commissions of $40,000 for the first year if he operates out of his home, half of which would be derived from his existing client base. Once the minimum required client base is developed, he could then move to another location.

Secondly, Charlotte could rent retail space in a local Bel Air shopping center at an amount of approximately $4,000 a month. The agency would have to be open seven days a week and evenings (under shopping center rules). This facility would require at least two agents and a receptionist/office manager. Charlotte forecasts that this location could generate 100 walk-ins per day, of which five could be converted to bookings. He also feels that bookings will be higher at this location than at any other due to the ability to attract street traffic, closeness to other stores, and the trading areas of adjacent stores.

The third option is to rent an office in the downtown business district. This office would be open during the week, Monday to Friday. An additional staff of at least two would be necessary, an agent and a receptionist/office assistant, with resulting salary and benefit expenses of $50,000 a year. Rent and other office expenses would run approximately $2,500 a month. It is projected that 50 visitors a week would walk into the office. Charlotte feels he can convert three of these walk-ins. This type of location would be ideal in attracting business travelers, but the average commission on domestic air travel is significantly less than on cruises.

Questions:

1.   Develop a methodology for estimating the trading area of each of these locations.

2.   Which location could be considered a parasite store? Explain your answer.

3.   Describe how Charlotte could assess the level of saturation of Bel Air in terms of travel agents.

4.   Which location do you recommend? Explain your answer.

CASE 24
Rehab Start: Location Matters

This case was prepared and written by Professor Denise T. Ogden, Penn State University, Lehigh Valley. Reprinted by permission.

Rehab Start is a retailer of rehabilitation products designed to help people with disabilities perform to their optimum ability. Rehab Start started in 2005 when one of the members of the board of directors of Astute Rehab hospital had an idea to raise money by selling items to patients and their families. Astute Rehab is a not-for-profit organization that relies on state funding, donations, and revenues from services. To launch Rehab Start, Astute Rehab initially used existing hospital gift store employees. After a few months, it realized that this operation needed a higher-level person to oversee its operations. Teresa Garcia, an executive with extensive experience in retailing, was ultimately hired.

Right from the beginning, Garcia wanted to make Rehab Start a destination store. After completing preliminary research, she confirmed her belief that there were no existing stores that served as a one-stop shop for rehabilitation products. Garcia's vision was to provide a wide product assortment of rehabilitation products to attract patients, as well as their families. Suitable merchandise included items for people in wheelchairs, for those with major vision restrictions, and products for children with physical limitations. The store also included items for the elderly.

The board of directors of the hospital placed lofty goals for the store to meet. Garcia felt these goals were unrealistic for a start-up business, but did not want to appear difficult by voicing her concerns. She knew that it would take at least three years for the store to be profitable, even though there was initial enthusiasm among the hospital staff, disabled persons, and their families.

Despite a strong merchandise assortment (90 percent of the people entering the store purchased at least one product), sales did not meet expectations. Garcia knew that customer traffic was a major concern and did everything possible to get more people into the store:

- Direct mail pieces were sent out to a targeted list of consumers.

- Advertising was placed in the local weekly newspaper.
- Events were also held at the store periodically to encourage traffic.

Although these tactics helped to some degree, sales did not increase as expected.

Garcia suspected that a major issue was the store's location. Rehab Start's retail store was located inside the Astute Rehab hospital, in a corner that received little customer traffic. In addition, the hospital's signage for the store is not prominent due to the restrictions placed by the board of directors. Not only is Rehab Start's location within the hospital a poor one, but the hospital facility is located several miles from the central business district. Due to the many turns and traffic obstacles, the store is very difficult to find. Garcia even got lost getting to her first interview.

Garcia initially believed the store's unique product assortment would make it a destination retailer and that location would not matter. As time went on, she realized that her initial perception was incorrect. In customer surveys, a major issue was getting to the store. Too often, shoppers noted that unless they were already at the hospital, they did not want to make the special trip to get to Rehab Start.

In an effort to increase sales, Garcia decided to launch a Web site. Once a few obstacles were cleared, the site was up and running. Sales increased dramatically in the first six months, and after just one year, half of Rehab Start's total sales were coming from the online channel. After the second year, 70 percent of total sales were from the online business. Rehab Start's online trading area also expanded internationally as word spread about its products.

Garcia made sure that online customer service matched the high level of customer service people experienced in the store. Although these results were promising, the overall store was not yet profitable. Next week, Garcia must answer to the board of directors.

The board is disappointed because the retail store is not fulfilling its expectations for revenues/profits. After two and a half years in business, Teresa Garcia is looking at options to keep Rehab Start running.

Questions:

1. Identify the requirements for a successful location for Rehab Start.

2. How can Teresa Garcia overcome the disadvantages inherent in Rehab Start's current location?

3. What are the synergies between Web retailing and bricks-and-mortar retailing for Rehab Start?

4. What mistakes, if any, did Teresa Garcia make in her initial assessment of Rehab Start?

5. Develop a short-range (three-year) plan to restore Rehab Start to profitability.

CASE 25

Sanchez Property Management

This case was prepared and written by Professor Michael R. Luthy, Bellarmine University. Reprinted by permission.

Sanchez & Sons Contractors recently completed construction of its newest property, the Desert Cactus Shopping Mall in Southwest Arizona. This is a fully-enclosed, three-level structure with a food court composed of six eateries and five anchor stores: Dillards, J.C. Penney, Best Buy, Famous Barr, and Toys "R" Us. Of the remaining 124 spaces for smaller individual stores, 95 are currently leased, and mall management is negotiating with several parties for the remaining ones. The physical layout of the facility is such that there is a large central open area on the ground floor (called the central galleria) that currently is envisioned as a rest area for mall patrons and will not be developed into stores.

Although the Desert Cactus facility will not have its official grand opening until the September 23-24, 2005 weekend, the property management firm operating the mall has received letters and telephone requests from the following groups to use Desert Cactus facilities:

- The Tucson chapter of the American Red Cross has asked to use the center court area for a three-day blood drive just prior to the Thanksgiving holiday in preparation for the additional blood needs the community will have during the Thanksgiving through New Year's period.

- The Salvation Army has requested permission to set up donation kettles with bell ringers at the major entrances to the mall during operating hours for 24 days starting December 1, 2005.

- A representative from Taos Junior High School has asked that foreign language classes from the school (French, Spanish, German, and Japanese) be allowed to sing holiday carols two evenings during the month of December in the mall's galleria as part of their class assignment.

- Several of the area's Boy Scouts of America troops are seeking permission to set up a staffed display booth during Scouting Week in October to attract new members and explain what Scouting is all about.

- The local Girl Scouts troop has asked permission to set up a booth to sell cookies to the public during its cookie/fundraising drive early next year.

- A local religious group has requested access to the mall to distribute literature and possibly solicit donations.

- Several local and regional fire departments would like to set up some displays in the mall during Fire Safety Week in September and want permission to use a portion of the parking lot for the Firefighters Olympics, which is a demonstration-oriented activity designed to educate the public as to what firefighters do.

Although the above requests are the only formal ones received to date, it is likely that other groups and organizations will approach mall management with similar requests.

Questions:

1. Should Sanchez management allow any non-tenant groups or organizations to use mall facilities? Explain your answer.

2. If it does, what kinds of activities should or should not be permitted?

3. What will be the costs to, and the responsibilities of, any groups or organizations allowed to use the facilities?

4. Should there be a maximum amount of time any one group or organization may use the facility in a given period (calendar year) or a limit to the number of groups using the facility at one time? Explain your answer.

5. How will you explain your new policy to tenants who may object?

CASE 26

Sports Motors

This case was prepared and written by Carolyn E. Predmore, Manhattan College, Port Washington, New York. Printed with permission.

Sports Motors is a privately owned car repair shop located in Nassau County, Long Island. While the shop's father and son owners (Joe and Vincent Fazio, respectively) prefer to work on high-end American and European vehicles, they can repair virtually any type of vehicle (including motorcycles). As a result of the shop's attention to detail, repairs are done right the first time, on schedule, and at the estimated cost. Other competitive advantages of Sports Motors include its mechanics' expansive knowledge of European and U.S. sports cars, a short waiting time for getting a car repaired (for some car dealerships, the waiting time is 1 to 2 weeks unless it is an extreme emergency such as a complete lack of brakes), and moderate repair prices (that are generally three-quarters of the prices charged by a new-car dealer).

A major strategic concern is the shop's need to expand its customer base to be able to keep Joe, Vincent, and two other full-time mechanics busy year round. It is not easy to find a skilled mechanic and once found, the Fazios need to keep the mechanic on a year-round basis. This past winter, there was barely enough revenue from repair work to cover the mechanics' salaries.

While repair work traditionally picks up once the snow melts, Joe is concerned about what to do the following winter.

The Fazios attribute the seasonal decline to several factors. One, the past year had an especially large snowfall. Many consumers with SUVs and other vehicles used the SUV exclusively and curtailed driving the other vehicles. Two, there has been an increase in the number of senior citizens that have moved into the area. Many of them are "snowbirds" who spend the winter months in Florida or in other warm locations.

One of the Fazios' clients, who is a marketing professor at a local college, offered to assess Sports Motors' retail strategy using the retail audit technique. Here are some of the major findings of the retail audit:

- The promotion for the shop includes listings in the Yellow Pages, and giveaways such as pens, key chains, and refrigerator magnets. Sports Motors could expand its promotional activities through using discount coupons in shopping circulars, by advertising on local radio stations, and by supporting local sports teams.

- Many new car dealers provide their customers with free loaner cars while their car is serviced or drive customers home or to a nearby train station. The Fazios do not provide such services. These services are important for customers without an extra car.

- While the Fazios stand behind their work, they do not provide a written guarantee of their repair work on the repair receipt.

- The appearance of the shop and office is unattractive. The repair area is typically cluttered and dirty. There is also no attractive waiting area with magazines, newspapers, televisions, and coffee. The professor commented that women customers would especially find the waiting area to be repulsive.

- Sports Motors needs to determine the market prices of other similar car repair shops in a five-mile area. While the owners assume that they have the lowest prices, they should be able to document that contention.

Questions:

1. Since Sports Motors has been successful for 32 years, does it still make sense for the owners to do a retail audit? Why or why not?

2. Several repair facilities will give a limited written guarantee for the service and repair provided. Should Sports Motors consider giving some limited warranty on its written receipt? Why or why not?

3. Customer service can be enhanced in many ways. What are some ways that Sports Motors could enhance its customer service?

4. What new auto-based accessories should Sports Motors consider to reduce its seasonality?

CASE 27

Sprucetown: Wrapping Civic Engagement into a Holiday Fashion Event

This case was prepared and written by Professor Constance Ulasewicz, San Francisco State University Reprinted by permission.

The Sprucetown shopping center is located in a metropolitan area adjacent to a major university. The mall's managing agent is aware that many of its shoppers and store employees are university students and often thought it would be a good idea to utilize their talents. One semester, a marketing professor from the university contacted the mall's management to determine if the mall would be interested in collaborating on a fashion show to kick off the holiday shopping season. The fashion show would take the place of the traditional tree trimming and lighting activity.

After much discussion between the mall's management and student group leaders, both groups decided to partner with a national nonprofit organization that helped local organizations provide coats to poor people within their communities. One of the locations for local residents to drop off used, but clean and wearable, coats would be the Sprucetown mall. The university students worked with Girl Scout leaders to develop a plan that would include Girl Scout involvement in the show. Students were also given the opportunity to work with the mall's marketing director in developing the fashion show. The Sprucetown management agent acted as a liaison between the university students and the retailers. Directly before the planned fashion show, the mall's manager increased its advertising and publicity efforts. A local graphic artist was hired to design the program's cover and mall signage. Students also sent out press releases to local news stations and newspapers.

The show was to include five scenes, be 35 minutes long, and include merchandise from 15 mall retailers. College students were to model the clothing for all of the scenes; some store employees also participated in the fashion show. One of the five scenes began with an explanation of the history and purpose of the nonprofit coat collection campaign. Girl Scouts in uniforms would be the first on the runway for this scene so their organization would gain recognition. There would also be additional commentary of how community residents could donate coats to the campaign. Sprucetown management and the Girl Scout leaders were pleased with the recognition for the coat collection campaign generated by local news stations and newspapers.

The day before the event, the runway was set up in the center court of the mall in anticipation of the show's 400 to 500 viewers. What happened next came as a surprise and disappointment to all. Many corporate retailers who had originally been asked to participate, but had declined, now demanded participation. While some stated that they just received corporate approval, others claimed they had inquired regarding participating, but the students had never followed up with them. Several stores also complained that the runway blocked physical access to their stores and

89

were concerned over the potential loss of revenues. The Sprucetown management office was filled with angry retail managers. A decision needed to be made whether to go on with the show or cancel the event.

Questions:

1. What could have been done to prevent the anger of some retailers?

2. Did the students intentionally not include retailers or was favoritism shown? Explain your answer.

3. Should the runway be moved or shortened? Explain your answer.

CASE 28

SweatyBetty

This case was prepared and written by Professor Leigh Sparks, University of Stirling, Scotland. Reprinted by permission.

There are many ways for sporting goods retailers to attract customers to visit their stores, make purchases, and to keep coming back. However, not all consumers will be attracted by the same stimuli. Some consumers will be turned off by a retailer's in-store environment or the type, range, price, and quality of the merchandise. There are also trends in consumers' perceptions, desires, and life stages that affect the level and nature of demand. For example, the positive feelings towards sporting goods retailers by young teenagers may be remarkably strong, but these feelings are reduced during later teenage years as participation rates in various sports decline.

There are also important differences between the sexes in terms of perceptions of sporting goods retailers. These differences are important because of the increasing scale of the female sports market, as well as the significant role women play in the purchase of sports products for males. Many sporting goods retailers are perceived by females as threatening environments that are "overly male." A typical comment by female shoppers is that "most sporting goods stores smell of stale sweat and old rubber and have the music turned up way too loud." Many females also view the typical sporting goods store's displays (which are commonly organized by activity such as golf, jogging, or swimming) as male-based.

Some brands have recognized and reacted to the issues that have been raised by these concerns. Nike, for example, has developed NIKEGoddess (recently renamed Nikewomen) to focus exclusively on the female sporting goods market. These stores have different colors, layouts, changing rooms, lighting, and product presentations than the typical Nike store. Nike also has developed a female-based Web site. http://nikewomen.nike.com/nikewomen/.

90

SweatyBetty (www.sweatybetty.com) is a young, small, London-based women-only retailer that can be classified as an "activewear boutique." The first SweatyBetty store opened in November 1998; there are now 10 stores with an average floor space of 700 square feet, as well as a department inside Selfridges in London and a transactional Web site that accounts for about 5 percent of total sales.

SweatyBetty is best described as a niche activewear chain, selling clothing and footwear for yoga, the beach, skiing, and the gym in addition to exercise-related accessories. It has a highly targeted product offering that provides a stylish, attractive, feminine range of clothing that is intended for exercise but looks good generally. Both super brands (such as Nike and Adidas) and niche brands (such as Pure Lime, Venice Beach and CandidaFaria) are sold. Endorsement by such celebrities as Elle MacPherson and Emma Bunton have raised the profile of the retailer. The retailer's offerings are targeted at the busy young mother with an active home life, as well as the young professional woman who works hard and has a high level of disposable income to spend on looking and feeling good.

The store's founders believe that they have identified a gap in the market for women-only activewear, arguing that many sports retailers were not meeting women's needs. For many women, the "feel-good" factor and the overall health and well-being aspects of keeping fit were more important than winning at a competitive activity. SweatyBetty aims to position itself as a confidant or friend, someone to provide advice and guide exercisers in the right direction. According to Tamara Hill-Norton, one of the chain's founders, "Why should women have to get advice on, or buy, a sports bra from a spotty male teenager?"

SweatyBetty's values and beliefs statement aptly describes the company:

- We believe in healthy living, having fun, and cool tracksuits.
- We welcome customers to share the SweatyBetty experience with us and to become our friends.
- We give our customers trusted advice and will deliver the perfect solution or even a magical transformation.
- A visit to SweatyBetty is sometimes unexpected, often memorable, but always satisfying.
- Our products look gorgeous and perform well. We like comfort, great value, and the WOW factor!
- We work with friends, we give each other support, and achieve a balanced life. We aim to keep things simple and to stay in control.
- We value financial stability and growth so that we can share the SweatyBetty experience as widely as possible.
- We are building an amazing company, run by women for women to be the best!!!

The store's atmospherics are based on the founders' beliefs that the typical sporting goods stores are too male and threatening for many female shoppers. SweatyBetty's stores are intensely feminine with soft lighting, spacious environments, and fixtures that resemble those found in upscale clothing stores. The stores are painted with white ceilings and loads of pink (also seen on its Web site). SweatyBetty's try-on rooms are spacious and feature large mirrors. The store's background music is soft and the overall atmosphere can be described as quiet and hushed.

A vital aspect of the store is its high levels of customer service. SweatyBetty's employees are carefully selected to reflect the store's target customers. Many of the employees are sports enthusiasts, who keep themselves fit and lead active lives. They are personified as "Betties" on the retailer's Web site. The shop staff is trained to know the store's products, as well as their appropriate use.

SweatyBetty plans to expand the number of stores in the London area and then to consider other urban areas in the United Kingdom. Store expansion is necessary to generate the appropriate scale needed to improve profitability. The founders recognize two significant problems associated with the necessary expansion. SweatyBetty will need to implement a series of financial controls to oversee a large, geographically dispersed business. SweatyBetty's founders are also concerned as to how the store can implement its corporate culture as it grows.

Questions:

1. How do women shop differently from men for sports products? How can these differences in consumer behavior be reflected in SweatyBetty's stores?

2. Evaluate the pros and cons of SweatyBetty's overall retail strategy.

3. What can other retailers learn from studying SweatyBetty's retail strategy?

4. Develop a series of financial controls for SweatyBetty to implement as it grows.

CASE 29

The Value Equation

This case was prepared and written by Professor Neill Crowley, St. Joseph's University, Philadelphia, Pennsylvania. Reprinted by permission.

Frank Murphy looked out the window of his office pondering his next steps. Murphy Mart had started as a one-store supermarket 35 years ago by Frank's father, John. Murphy Mart had now grown to a "chain" of 20 stores operating in two states.

Murphy Mart owed most of its success to its treatment of customers. John Murphy and now his son, Frank, had prided themselves on the firm's ability to ingratiate itself with its customers. This effort to "delight the customer" was the result of relentless efforts to focus on the customer by:

- Hiring practices that resulted in selecting employees on the basis of their customer interaction skills.

- Continuous auditing through mystery shoppers and other metrics of customer satisfaction levels. Incentives and rewards were given to full and part-time employees who achieved specific levels and/or instances of "customer delight."

- Paying a great deal of attention to the "customer delights" incentives and rewards program. Interviews among existing, as well as employees who recently had left the company, showed a high awarcness and appreciation of the "customer delights" program. Many of the existing employees pointed to this employee recognition/ incentive program as a major reason for their length of employment.

- Murphy Mart was generally recognized as one of the leaders in its training "investment" per employee. It invested heavily in customer service training. It was not uncommon for each employee to receive anywhere from two to four weeks of training a year. Much of the training was designed to give employees the necessary product knowledge designed to enable them to impart knowledge to the customer about the store's products, food preparation and menu planning, and nutrition information.

While Murphy Mart paid competitive wages and reasonable benefits to its employees, their total compensation was at the low end of the scale for comparable work in other supermarket chains.

Apart from its rigorous emphasis on "delighting" the customer, Murphy Mart had no other notable attributes relative to supermarket selection and usage. The term "average" appeared most applicable when judging Murphy Mart's other offerings. The "average" tag that was attached to Murphy Mart was now a top concern for Frank Murphy. Frank had just been informed that within eighteen to twenty-four months, not one but two 150,000-square-foot food and nonfood supercenters would be opening in two of Murphy Mart's trading areas. Frank Murphy knew that while he had to keep his stores up to date relative to equipment and technology, they would be unable to compete on a size and, perhaps more importantly, a price basis with these huge supercenters.

Jim Bates, Murphy Mart's sales manager, had also been studying ways to address the supercenter challenge. Jim had just returned from a seminar dealing with customer value. One of the speakers put forth the argument that value for the customer was a function of several variables and that value could be expressed using one of the following equations:

Value = variety/assortment + convenience + service + quality + price + store ambiance

or

Value = low cost producer + superior technology + quality service excellence

The speaker pointed out that while no retailer could excel at all of the variables listed in either equation, the "best" retailers were clearly superior on at least one or perhaps two or three of the equation variables. Indeed, some "best-of-class" retailers had developed one or two of the variables into a sustainable competitive advantage.

Jim Bates discussed "working" the "value equation" with Frank Murphy. Frank thought the value equation concept made sense but was unable to think about how it could be used to enhance Murphy Mart's competitive perception with its customers. He challenged Jim Bates to give him specifics on using the value equation to help Murphy Mart hold its business in view of the looming competitive threat.

Questions:

1.   Evaluate Murphy Mart's overall human resource strategy.

2.   Discuss the differences in value based on both equations.

3.   Describe four possible sustainable competitive advantages for Murphy Mart to pursue. Assess each strategy.

4.   How can Murphy Mart best compete against the supercenter?

CHAPTER-BASED EXERCISES

CHAPTER 1 EXERCISE

Distribution Decisions for a New Electronics Store

The owner of a new electronics store is uncertain with regard to several distribution decisions, including these:

- Should merchandise be purchased directly from manufacturers or should a major wholesaler be sought out?
- What assortment of brand names and models should be carried?
- What kind of promotion should be used?
- Who should be responsible for storing, shipping, and price-marking merchandise?
- What kind of support (e.g., advertising, displays, etc.) should be expected from suppliers?
- Should exclusive, intensive, or selective relationships with suppliers be sought?
- How should store fixture suppliers be selected?

The store owner has hired you to help with these decisions.

Questions:

1. What information must you obtain from the store owner before making any suggestions?

2. What criteria would you consider for each of the decision areas noted in this exercise before making recommendations?

CHAPTER 2 EXERCISE

Brian Laine Insurance: Planning a Service Business

Brian Laine worked for Prudential Insurance as a salesman for eight years after graduating from college, and enjoyed all of them. However, he reached the point where opening an independent insurance company became important. So, in 1998, Laine opened his own company. Because of the firm's small size and unknown name, he realized he would have trouble selling commercial insurance and decided to concentrate on homeowners' insurance.

In the beginning, Laine selected names from a local telephone directory to solicit business. Although progress was slow, this endeavor proved profitable by 2000, especially with renewals and referrals. During this time, Laine concentrated on advertising in the Yellow Pages and newspapers and appeared before local civic and consumer groups. Several group life-insurance plans developed out of these appearances.

Laine encouraged homeowners to buy all their insurance from him, and many did. He has also taken pride in promptly answering all phone calls, in following up with his insurance companies, and in suggesting additional coverage based on life cycle changes that affect each client (e.g., the birth of a child or a client's need to consider retirement planning).

During late 2004, premiums reached the point where Brian was able to match his previous income with Prudential. In fact, Laine is now facing these lucrative alternatives: (1) to open a large office and hire a full-time staff; (2) to merge with a slightly larger company; or (3) to bring his accounts with him and return to work as a salesman at Prudential.

Questions:

1. Has Brian Laine done a good job of planning his service strategy? Explain your answer.

2. How can Laine better utilize the principles of relationship retailing?

3. Develop a customer service strategy for Brian Laine.

4. What are the pros and cons of each of the alternatives now confronting Brian Laine?

Student's Name _____
Class/Section _____
Instructor _____

CHAPTER 3 EXERCISE

Strategy Review of a Top 100 U.S.-Based Retailer

This case was prepared and written by Professor Phyllis Fein, Westchester Community College, Valhalla, New York. Reprinted by permission.

You have been hired as a consultant to review the overall strategy of a top 100 U.S.-based retailer.

STEP 1: RESEARCH (2 pages)
Include all of the key facts about the retailer including its history, sales and profit growth, corporate mission, and important financial data from the retailer's annual report and balance sheet. Also include examples of advertising and important events that shaped the company.

STEP 2: CONDUCT A SWOT ANALYSIS (1 page)
Conduct a SWOT analysis to identify <u>internal</u> strengths and weaknesses of the retailer, as well as <u>external</u> threats and opportunities associated with the industry, competition, customers, etc.

Use the following grid to list your SWOT analysis:

Strengths	Weaknesses	Opportunities	Threats

STEP 3: CHOOSE A KEY COMPETITOR AND PREDICT THEIR FUTURE (2 pages)
Compare your retailer with an important key competitor. Note important differences and similarities in strategy. What can your retailer learn from its competitors' successes and failures?

STEP 4: RECOMMENDATIONS FOR MAKING YOUR RETAIL CLIENT BIGGER AND BETTER (1 Page)

Differentiate between short term, immediate term, and long-term strategies. Develop strategies that are aggressive, as well as conservative. Also develop strategies that require significant investments, as well as those that require few funds.

APPENDIX
Include copies of your research such as articles, Web links, copies of a retailer's current advertising, etc.

CHAPTER 4 EXERCISE

Aerobics Unlimited: Evaluating Two Franchisees

Aerobics Unlimited is a franchisor with 45 outlets in the Eastern United States. Its franchises have been considered an attractive investment by franchisees for a variety of reasons: its good reputation and proven track record, availability of company assistance, and low initial investment ($5,000 to $15,000) versus several hundred thousand dollars or more for a hamburger franchise. In one large state, the average Aerobic Unlimited franchise recently reported profits of about $40,000 (excluding the owner's salary).

Despite the overall success of Aerobics Unlimited, the firm has had some failures among its franchisees. Common problems leading to franchise failures are the franchisee giving up on a store location too quickly, lack of good instructors, low dedication to the store, not complying with company requirements, etc. In contrast, successful franchisees have hard-working owners, who are persistent and strictly adhere to company policies.

Exhibit 1 shows the characteristics of a successful and unsuccessful franchise operation.

Exhibit 1
A Successful Versus an Unsuccessful Aerobics Unlimited Franchise
(during a recent year)

	Successful Outlet	Unsuccessful Outlet
Income:	$ 455,000	$ 257,000
Expenses:		
Owner's salary	30,000	30,000
Payroll	144,500	90,000
Rent, property tax	38,750	38,000
Royalty (rent override)	15,300	8,600
Franchise fees (advertising)	63,000	28,200
Utilities and sanitation	28,800	18,250
Taxes and insurance	19,650	14,300
Maintenance and repair	20,800	12,500
Interest	17,600	5,000
Depreciation	23,000	12,000
Miscellaneous	15,400	7,500
Total expenses	$ 416,800	$ 264,350
Profit (loss)	$ 38,200	$ (7,350)

Questions:

1.   What are the advantages of an Aerobics Unlimited franchise in comparison with operating an independent aerobics business?

2.   Evaluate Exhibit 1.

3.   What suggestions can you make to Aerobics Unlimited (as the franchisor) based on Exhibit 1?

4.   What are the risks of becoming an Aerobics Unlimited franchisee?

Student's Name _____
Class/Section _____
Instructor _____

CHAPTER 5 EXERCISE

A Traditional Department Store Decides to Confront Off-Price Chains

Dennison's is a traditional department store chain located in suburban Cleveland that is confronting heavy competition from off-price chains. In recent years, a number of developments have occurred which have caused the store's apparel division merchandise manager to be especially concerned:

- The number of off-price chains within 4 miles of Dennison's main store has recently increased to five. In addition, the move to better locations by some off-price chains is threatening several of its branches' apparel business.
- The off-price chains are becoming more aggressive in buying. In some instances, they are contracting with manufacturers for current season merchandise instead of concentrating on irregulars, end-of-season goods, and odd lots.
- A number of customers have complained that some merchandise sold at Dennison's can be found at a 30 to 40 percent savings elsewhere. While Dennison's will match any store's price for identical merchandise, it is concerned about how long it can continue this practice.

The division merchandise manager has been asked to draw up a plan to respond to the increased competition from off-price chains. Among the options to be considered are as follows:

- Refusing to buy from merchants who sell the same goods to off-price chains.
- Focusing on high fashion and on Dennison's fashion leadership niche.
- Increasing service levels and store atmosphere appeals.
- Competing head-on with discounters through special sales, clearance centers, and early markdowns.

Questions:

1. What advantages does Dennison's have in comparison to off-price chains?

2. Should Dennison's continue to match off-price chain pricing on identical merchandise when a customer complains? Explain your answer.

3. Evaluate each alternative strategy.

4. Which strategy should Dennison's pursue? Why?

CHAPTER 6 EXERCISE

Tops Luggage: Planning and Implementing a Web Site

Tops is a luggage manufacturer that has sold much of its luggage on a private-label basis to large chain-based luggage retailers and major department stores. While Tops' luggage features high-quality construction and materials (such as fabric, zippers, and wheels), the Tops brand has no recognition since its retailer customers use their own brand designation on Tops' products.

Tops is now planning a Web site to sell luggage under its own brand. Tops assumes that the site will give it access to additional geographic markets, will help develop its brand name, and will reduce dependency on several key accounts.

Tops' site will feature two of Tops' most popular models: a valet pack which enables a user to store two jackets and slacks on a hanger, and a carry-on luggage model featuring wheels made from in-line skate components and multiple compartments. Tops plans to promote its Web site through one-page ads in magazines with major travel-related magazines. The ads will feature testimonials from airline crews as to the durability of Tops' luggage.

Tops plans to include the following on its Web site:
- The history of the company.
- A description of the materials used and construction details for its models.
- A color chart.
- An order form with an easy-to-use shopping cart.
- A listing of important travel-related sites such as airline listings, weather reporting, and so on.

Questions:

1. What are the pros and cons of Tops' proposed retail strategy?

2. Develop suggestions for improving Tops' proposed site using the following criteria: cross merchandising, customer service, free shipping, one-click ordering, and selection.

3. How can Tops avoid channel conflict with its current retailer customers due to its proposed multi-channel strategy?

Student's Name _____
Class/Section _____
Instructor _____

CHAPTER 7 EXERCISE

Shopping Journal

This case was prepared and written by Professor Phyllis Fein, Westchester Community College, Valhalla, New York. Reprinted by permission.

TIME TO SHOP AGAIN!!!

Over the next week, keep a shopping log of any and all of your purchases—from gum to a computer. Write down the purchase description, date, place of purchase, and each step of your decision process that led to you making each purchase. Use as many pages as you need to keep track of your purchases. Now, try to think back on the reason you purchased what you did–going through the steps on page 202 in the text. Next, try to categorize just what type of purchase it was based on your decision-making process:

- Limited decision making
- Extended decision making
- Routine decision making
- Impulse purchase

How did you feel afterwards (your post-purchase behavior)?

NOTE: You can also interview your friends and family about their recent purchases—but make sure to indicate who made the purchase!!

Your Purchase	Type of Purchase	Purchase/Post-Purchase Behavior
(1)		
(2)		
(3)		
(4)		
(5)		
(6)		

CHAPTER 8 EXERCISE

A Jewelry Store Turns to Research

Walter Kravat worked as a manager for a major jewelry store chain until two years ago when he started his own store. Situated in a high-traffic neighborhood shopping center, the store has a new storefront, display cases, fixtures, and carpeting. Walter has positioned the store as a full-service, full-markup retailer. Besides Walter and two salespersons, the store has a full-time jeweler who is responsible for repairs, jewelry redesigning, and insurance appraisals. The store is an authorized dealer for a wide selection of watch brands such as Seiko, Pulsar, Movado, etc.

After being in business for two years, the store has not met sales expectations. Walter, after talking in-depth with several friends, feels that several factors may be jointly responsible for the lack of success.

First, consumers are likely to judge a jeweler's pricing policy based on discounts offered on watches. Walter discounts Seiko and Pulsar brands by 10 percent. Department stores typically offer these brands at 20 to 25 percent off list during special sales. Furthermore, many discount houses feature "gray market" items (watches not imported or guaranteed by the U.S. authorized importer of these brands) at 50 percent or even more off list. Walter will not stock these "gray market" watches, since they were not designed for the U.S. market and will not be repaired by the official U.S. importer.

Second, department and discount stores in Walter's area are very aggressive in their jewelry advertising. In many cases, however, their standard prices are no lower than Walter's regular selling prices. Nevertheless, these stores are significant competitors due to their credibility and offering of money-back privileges (Walter allows exchanges but no cash refunds).

Third, operating one store does not allow Walter to use media available to department stores and discount stores.

Walter wants to research the feasibility of the following three strategies that he feels may help increase sales:

- To create store traffic through the use of special promotions. One week per month, the store would feature special purchases, markdowns on slow-moving merchandise, etc.
- To develop a "designer selection." This will consist of antique, estate, and one-of-a-kind jewelry and watches.
- To become more price aggressive by quoting prices on the phone, allowing bargaining, and matching department store sale prices.

The strategy selected will be based on marketing research findings. Walter is willing to pay a consultant $500 per day for up to 7 days plus up to $5,000 for expenses in conjunction with the study.

Questions:

1. Develop a marketing research proposal to present to Walter.

2. Outline project costs and time requirements for your research proposal.

3. Develop a questionnaire to define the problem area and evaluate alternative strategies.

4. Describe how you plan to analyze the data from the questionnaire responses.

Student's Name _____
Class/Section _____
Instructor _____

CHAPTER 9 EXERCISE

Trading-Area Analysis for a Home Improvement Chain

Made-to-Last Paint is a 25-store home improvement chain featuring paint, hardware, lumber, do-it-yourself supplies, and seasonal goods.

The chain's stores span four counties in two states; the distance between the two furthest stores is about 80 miles. All stores are located in affluent suburban areas. Generally, stores are in freestanding locations with ample parking.

Made-to-Last Paint is in the process of re-examining its trading-area strategy as a result of a preliminary analysis by a retail consultant. Part of the consultant's report follows:

"There appears to have been no rational strategy on which store locations have been based. Among my preliminary findings are:

- *High waste in advertising. About 25 percent of the readers of the firm's major newspaper for advertising, The Daily Sun, live further than 7 miles from the closest Made-to-Last Paint store.*
- *Many poorly performing stores could have been identified prior to their opening. Three of seven poorly performing stores are located in areas with large concentrations of apartment houses and cooperatives. Dwellers in these units are not inclined to purchase paint, hardware, lawn supplies, and snow removal tools. Another store is the sole unit in its state. Two other units are located in extremely affluent areas served by landscape gardeners, carpenters, and general contractors instead of do-it-yourselfers.*
- *Executives in the firm are unfamiliar with census tract data."*

The firm is now convinced that it needs to regularly use trading-area analysis. It also realizes that an overall evaluation may involve store elimination in some markets and store expansion in others.

Questions:

1.   How would trading-area analysis differ for a chain and independent retailer?

2.   What are the steps that Made-to-Last Paint should pursue in evaluating its trading areas?

3.   What characteristics of trading areas would you assume would be associated with success for Made-to-Last Paint? Explain your answer.

4.   Is the *Census of Population* a more appropriate source of trading-area data than the *American Community Survey* for Made-to-Last Paint? Explain your answer.

Student's Name _____
Class/Section _____
Instructor _____

CHAPTER 10 EXERCISE

Site Evaluation Checklist

This case was prepared and written by Professor Phyllis Fein, Westchester Community College, Valhalla, New York. Reprinted by permission.

SITE EVALUATION CHECKLIST
Due Date: _____

Choose your favorite retail store, hangout, diner, etc and <u>you</u> decide how well it measures up in the following Location/Site Evaluation Checklist. (See Figure 10-7 in the text). After your thorough evaluation, think about what you would change, if you could, about the site location of your favorite place.

YOUR FAVORITE PLACE: _____
WHY?_____

LOCATION: _____

CRITERIA	EXPLANATION	DETAILS/ DESCRIPTION	RATING: 1-10 (10 being excellent, 1 being the worst)
1. Pedestrian Traffic	❑ Number of people (count on average/day) ❑ Type of People		
2. Vehicular Traffic	❑ Number of vehicles ❑ Type of vehicles ❑ Traffic congestion		
3. Parking Facilities	❑ Number and quality of parking spots ❑ Distance to store ❑ Availability of employee Parking		
4. Transportation	❑ Availability of mass transit (trains, buses) ❑ Access from major highways ❑ Ease of deliveries		
5. Store Composition	❑ Number and size of stores ❑ Retail balance		

CRITERIA	EXPLANATION	DETAILS/ DESCRIPTION	RATING: 1-10 (10 being excellent, 1 being the worst)
6. Specific Site	❑ Visibility ❑ Placement in the location (good spot?) ❑ Size and shape of the lot ❑ Size and shape of the building ❑ Condition and age of the lot and building		
7. Terms of Occupancy	❑ Ownership ❑ Zoning restrictions ❑ Number and size of stores		
8. Overall Rating	❑ General location ❑ Specific site		

NOW...WHAT WOULD YOU CHANGE???

Student's Name _____
Class/Section _____
Instructor _____

CHAPTER 11 EXERCISE

Human Resources Management

This case was prepared and written by Professor Phyllis Fein, Westchester Community College, Valhalla, New York. Reprinted by permission.

Management Interview/Hiring Criteria
Due Date: _____

THIS IS A TWO-STEP ASSIGNMENT:

STEP 1: You have been just hired as Senior Personnel Director. Employee morale is down, turnover is high, and you need to find out why. Using the following questions as a guideline, interview an actual retail manager from a local retailer to help predict employee motivation and satisfaction.

You will need to attach his/her business card and include the signature of the manager you interviewed.

NAME OF RETAIL MANAGER: _____

TITLE: _____
SIGNATURE: _____

STORE NAME AND LOCATION: _____

1. How long have you been working at this store? For this company?

2. What is your current position?

3. How many hours do you work?

4. How many employees do you supervise?

5. List some of your duties and responsibilities.

6. Do you like the kind of work you do?

7. Does your work give you a sense of accomplishment?

8. How does the amount of work you are expected to do influence your overall attitude about your job? Your company?

---

9. How do your physical working conditions influence your overall attitude about your job?

10. Do you feel good about the future of your company?

11. Do you think your company/stores are making the changes necessary to compete effectively?

12. Describe your career goals.

ATTACH BUSINESS CARD HERE

STEP 2: You are a recent college graduate looking for a challenging retail position. Go to a retail organization and determine what skills it is looking for in new retail employees by filling out a job application. Write a brief job description of the job you "applied for" and attach the actual job application to this assignment.

CHAPTER 12 EXERCISE

Operating Noble's House

Ed and Virginia Noble own and operate a small gardening supplies store called Noble's House in a middle-class suburban area. The Nobles have been in business for seven years and have made a moderate profit, in addition to their combined annual salaries of $75,000, each year.

As of this date, Noble's House has these balance sheet data:
- Current liabilities of $75,000
- Current assets of $40,000
- Fixed assets of $225,000
- Fixed liabilities of $50,000

The net sales for this year are expected to be $225,000. After deducting for the cost of goods sold and various operating expenses, net profit should be 8 percent of sales. Of particular concern to the Nobles is their store's cash flow projections. While during peak seasons cash flow is very positive, in January and February, it is quite unsatisfactory (due to low sales levels and the need to make Spring purchases).

Questions:

1. What is the net worth of Noble's House? Comment on this.

2. Calculate asset turnover, profit margin, and financial leverage for Noble's House. Explain your findings.

3. Compute the return on net worth and the return on assets for Noble's House. Explain your findings.

4. How can Noble's House reduce its cash flow problems?

Student's Name _____
Class/Section _____
Instructor _____

CHAPTER 13 EXERCISE

Developing a Crisis Management Plan

As director of operations for a home improvement chain, you have been asked to develop a crisis management plan for a number of contingencies. The store's management has directed you to develop plans for the following contingencies: loss of power due to a hurricane or other natural disaster, the sudden resignation or illness of a key employee, and a key supplier going bankrupt.

Each plan needs to:
- Communicate the situation to all affected parties. This should include vendors, current customers, future customers, the general public, government agencies, and so on.
- Identify the chain of command for each crisis. For example, the retailer's director of information technology should be in charge of problems relating to the firm's Web site, while the retailer's director of security needs to direct operations involving store theft.
- Develop a strategy to minimize the potential loss in sales and profits.

Questions:

1.   Develop a crisis management plan for loss of power due to a hurricane.

2.   Develop a crisis management plan for the sudden death, disability, or resignation of a key employee.

3.   Develop a crisis management plan for a key supplier going bankrupt.

Student's Name _____
Class/Section _____
Instructor _____

CHAPTER 14 EXERCISE

Private Branding at a Major Computer Retailer

A major computer retailer is considering developing a private brand for its desktop computers, modems, monitors, disks, and related supplies. To increase credibility for these products, the retailer will provide extended warranties at low cost for these products. The retailer will also work with its vendors to ensure that specifications for these products will be of high quality. All private-label products will be subjected to rigorous testing in both laboratory and field-based environments.

The retailer feels that there are a number of major benefits to this strategy:

- Many of the retailer's smaller vendors have no brand image. The private-label brand of the retailer would establish greater credibility to these products.

- If the private-brand strategy is successful, the retailer could encourage consumers to become store loyal due to brand loyalty.

- Many small vendors would be happy to private label their output subject to the retailer's specifications. This assures the vendor of large purchases. Furthermore, private-label purchases cannot be returned to the vendor due to poor sales.

- Due to large quantity purchases and savings in promotional costs, these private-label products would represent excellent value to the customer.

- The private label strategy would reduce price competition among these products. Consumers could not request price matching on private-label goods.

Questions:

1. What are the pros and cons of the retailer's private-brand strategy?

2. What additional tactics does the retailer have to plan and implement to better ensure success? Explain your answer.

3. What strategies could a manufacturer brand implement to counter the private brand's success?

CHAPTER 15 EXERCISE

Competitive Shopping Report

This case was prepared and written by Professor Phyllis Fein, Westchester Community College, Valhalla, New York. Reprinted by permission.

Competitive Shopping Report
Due Date: _____

Your college bookstore has just decided to introduce a trendy new fashion department. You are the merchandise manager for this new department and have been assigned to develop the plan for only **ONE OF THE FOLLOWING FASHION PRODUCT CATEGORIES**:

- ✓ JEANS
- ✓ SNEAKERS
- ✓ WATCHES

Using the steps in the merchandise plan (Figure 15-1) go through the exercise of researching alternative brands, pricing, and image/positioning to then recommend a merchandise plan/assortment.

YOU MUST HAVE RESEARCH ON AT LEAST FIVE ALTERNATIVES AND ATTACH ALL OF YOUR RESEARCH—INCLUDING PRICING, BRAND LOGOS, ETC. THE INTERNET SITES OF POPULAR BRANDS WILL BE QUITE HELPFUL!!!!

Brand	Description/Image	Pricing

Brand	Description/Image	Pricing

YOUR MERCHANDISE ASSORTMENT:
(Include the percent of each brand and your rationale)

CHAPTER 16 EXERCISE

Men's Discount Clothing (MDC): Planning Monthly Purchases

Ben Jason owns Men's Discount Clothing (MDC), a store based in downtown Milwaukee, Wisconsin. The retailer buys imported suits, sport jackets, raincoats, and slacks. All garments have the MDC label, and all alterations are included in each garment's price. MDC's retail price lines are low to moderate, the firm advertises weekly in Milwaukee's major newspaper, and has a convenient location with ample parking.

In reviewing MDC's financial records, the firm's accountant has raised some concerns. The accountant feels that Ben is overly optimistic in forecasting sales. Ben defends this practice as due to uncertainty with delivery dates. To Ben, over ordering reduces the effects of slow delivery. The accountant would also like Ben to develop a yearly plan relating to sales, reductions, and inventory levels. Ben likes to plan only 1 to 2 months ahead due to inaccuracy with plans beyond this time period.

MDC's sales, reductions, and inventory levels for the most recent fiscal year are shown in Exhibit 1.

Exhibit 1
Men's Discount Clothing: Sales, Reductions, and Inventory Levels
(Most Recent Fiscal Year)

Month	Actual Retail Sales	Reductions	Beginning-of-Month Inv. Level (at Retail)	End-of-Month Inventory Level (at Retail)
January	$210,000	$ 20,000	$100,000	$ 80,000
February	190,000	30,000	80,000	150,000
March	350,000	10,000	150,000	100,000
April	250,000	10,000	100,000	100,000
May	260,000	10,000	100,000	25,000
June	470,000	15,000	25,000	150,000
July	220,000	40,000	150,000	90,000
August	140,000	20,000	90,000	150,000
September	290,000	10,000	150,000	120,000
October	220,000	12,000	120,000	250,000
November	420,000	30,000	250,000	300,000
December	510,000	30,000	300,000	150,000
Total Year	$3,530,000	$ 237,000		

Questions:

1. Based on Exhibit 1, what should MDC's planned purchases at retail have been each month?

2. If the firm has a 40 percent markup at retail, compute its open-to-buy at cost for each month.

3. Compute MDC's monthly inventory turnover.

4. Evaluate the accountant's arguments.

Student's Name _____
Class/Section _____
Instructor _____

CHAPTER 17 EXERCISE

Smith Appliances: Dealing with Intensive Price Competition

Smith Appliances is a major regional chain specializing in refrigerators, televisions, washing machines, stereos, and dishwashers. It has been established for over 30 years and is respected in the community. Its pricing strategy is to take normal markups, but to permit some bargaining by customers. In general, the store would not sell merchandise unless its markup at retail exceeds 15 percent. It now finds that it must re-examine its pricing strategy in light of several developments.

Smith Appliances recently has had significant competition from retailers who give price quotes on the phone. Typically, these retailers place ads in local papers stating they will beat any price. They have no retail store, no displays, and prefer to stock only high-turnover items. Generally, they will ship merchandise if a customer calls in his/her order with a credit-card deposit; goods are usually delivered within 2 to 3 days. All merchandise carries the manufacturers' full guarantee. Discounters' prices are 10 to 15 percent below Smith's.

In addition, the firm finds that its typical customer has now become more price conscious. This may be due to an extension of the influence of off-price chains on apparel and footwear, and to increased price advertising by Smith's traditional competitors. One major competitor actively promotes that it will "beat all advertised and quoted prices."

Smith Appliances is concerned about what pricing strategy to undertake in response to competitive developments. Some alternatives it is considering are:
- Do nothing. The firm is currently successful and should not erode profit margins.
- Focus on full service. Include such services as microwave cooking classes, washing machine and dryer hookup, and reduced installation charges for major appliances.
- Match all prices, provided the firm can verify price levels through phone calls or advertisement copy.

Questions:

1. Evaluate each alternative.

2. Which alternative strategy should Smith Appliances pursue?

3. How can Smith prevent shoppers from visiting its store; examining its product samples; getting product, feature, and warranty information; and then saving 10 to 15 percent by going to a discounter?

4. How should an appliance manufacturer react to increased retail price discounting? Distinguish between short- and long-term implications in your answer.

CHAPTER 18 EXERCISE

Betty's Dress Shop: Planning a Retail Image

Betty's Dress Shop has been at its present location for five years. The firm specializes in "off-the-rack," as well as custom-made dresses for use at weddings and other formal functions. Betty's Dress Shop is located in a strip location on a major thoroughfare. Neighboring stores are 7-Eleven and a discount candy/chocolate store.

Betty's Dress Shop's retail strategy is comprised of the following:

- A product mix of custom-made dresses (30 percent) and off-the-rack dresses (70 percent).
- All garments are sold with alterations included. An especially skilled fitter/tailor is on the premises.
- All off-the-rack dresses stocked have limited distribution. This limits price competition with department stores and other specialty stores in the area.
- The price line for "off-the-rack" dresses is between $500 and $750; the average dress purchase is $600.
- The firm has a low-key approach to selling. Sales personnel are paid on a salary basis and are encouraged to be honest about the appearance of each garment.

Nevertheless, Betty (the store owner) is concerned about the store's overall image. Her feelings are based on extended discussions with the store's customers and with local residents. Betty feels that many people are unaware of the store's existence. The store is set back from the thoroughfare due to zoning requirements; this gives the store poor visibility. The store also has poor affinities with neighboring stores.

The store has a cluttered appearance. This is due to several factors. One, no double-tiered racks are used. Two, when it is busy, store personnel have little time to put tried-on garments back on the racks. Three, the sewing machine and clothes-steaming machine are visible. Four, the store also sells sweaters, shorts, and costume jewelry. Lastly, the store has been put together piecemeal, as Betty could afford to make improvements. Thus, the store fixtures, carpeting color, clothes racks, and storefront are not coordinated.

Questions:

1. What should Betty do as a result of her preliminary feelings?

2. How could these problems be avoided?

3. Explain how Betty can determine her optimal space needs using the model stock and sales-productivity ratio approaches.

4. What factors should Betty consider in reassessing her customer service strategy?

CHAPTER 19 EXERCISE

Ellie's Leather Goods: Modifying a Promotion Strategy

Ellie Farmer owns a two-year-old leather goods store that features luggage, women's bags, and wallets. The store is situated in a community shopping center anchored by a junior department store in an affluent neighborhood. Its fixtures are chrome and glass and it utilizes plush carpeting and silver/black stripes on the walls. This outlet's customers are more knowledgeable, less susceptible to sales presentations, value conscious, style (fashion) conscious, more likely to comparison shop, and less likely to buy an item as a gift than those shopping at older, more traditional leather goods stores. Many unique, high-priced goods are carried at the store.

Until now, Ellie has relied on personal selling, in-store displays, special mailings to loyal customers, and word-of-mouth communication in her promotion strategy. But, Ellie believes the time is right to begin advertising. She is currently devising a strategy that takes these factors into account:

- The store is based on a full-service, fair-profit-margin concept. Personal service, a generous return policy, and repair services are provided.
- First-quality popular brands are carried. All products are genuine leather. No synthetics are sold.
- Ads should not be dominated by price. A "classy" look is necessary.
- While flyers and Pennysaver newspapers have excellent geographic fit for the store, garage sales, used furniture vendors, car washes, and others are advertising in these media.
- Customer demand is seasonal and varies by product category. For example, attaché cases are good gift items and have high holiday sales. Luggage is popular during May and June, as consumers prepare for vacations.
- Between $10,000 and $15,000 is available for yearly advertising.

Questions

1. Develop an overall promotion plan for Ellie's Leather Goods.

2. Develop a yearly media plan for Ellie Farmer. Explain your answer.

3. Which types of sales promotion should Ellie use at her store? Explain your answer.

4. How could Ellie determine the effectiveness of her new promotion plan?

CHAPTER 20 EXERCISE

Application of SERVQUAL

This case was prepared and written by Professor Phyllis Fein, Westchester Community College, Valhalla, New York. Reprinted by permission.

You are a customer shopping for the same exact product or service at two different retailers. Try to visit each retailer at least twice. For example, purchase a cup of coffee at Starbucks and one at a local diner. Make sure the product or service is the same, but that the two retailers are very different!!!

Now, for each shopping experience, rate the following key factors that affected your total retailing experience:
- Reliability: providing services as promised, performing services right the first time.
- Responsiveness: keeping customers informed about when services will be done.
- Assurance: employees who instill consumer confidence and make them feel secure.
- Empathy: providing individual attention in a caring way.
- Tangibles: modern equipment and appealing facilities.

Rating: 1-10; 10 being the best, 1 being the worst. Remember, use your experience to form your opinion, not the opinions you had before you went shopping!!!

YOUR PRODUCT: _____

Factor	Shopping Trip #1 (Detail your experience with each factor.)	Shopping Trip #2 (Detail your experience with each factor.)
Reliability		
Responsiveness		
Assurance		
Empathy		
Tangibles		

Integrative Exercise

Planning an Overall Retail Strategy for a New Retail Store

This case was prepared and written by Professor Phyllis Fein, Westchester Community College, Valhalla, New York. Reprinted by permission.

In this seven-part assignment, students are required to meet as a team and go through all of the steps in developing and implementing a retail strategy that will end in the creation of a retail business.

ASSIGNMENT #	Team Assignments		Due Date	Grade
	Topic:	**Lesson:**		
1	Team Self-Assessment and Business Choice	Analyze the first step in strategic planning, the situation analysis for starting a new business.		
2 Cpt 3	Competitive Analysis/ Positioning Map	Apply key principles of product/benefit positioning to the competitive environment.		
3 Cpt 7	Customer Demographic/ Lifestyle Analysis	Identify the key elements of a customer profile and shopping behavior influences.		
4 Cpt 10	Location/Layout	Evaluate and apply the criteria for retail site and location selection to your new store.		
5 Cpt 12	Pricing/Financial Goals	Apply assumptions about the financial objectives of your retail business to a financial plan—a profit-and-loss statement.		
6 Cpt H	Merchandise Plan	Using results from assignments 1 to 5, analyze and recommend the best merchandising assortment for your store.		
7 Cpt 16	Shopping Bag/Store Image/Promotion— Final Presentation	Apply the key principles of positioning to the consumer to a fully developed store concept and opening event.		
TOTAL	Total semester average= All assignment grades/7			

TEAM ASSIGNMENT #1: Team Self-Assessment and Business Choice
Due Date: _____

RETAIL MANAGEMENT TEAM NUMBER: _____

Team Players: Strengths and Weaknesses of Planned Store:

1. _____   _____

2. _____   _____

3. _____   _____

4. _____   _____

5. _____   _____

6. _____   _____

Team Players: Strengths and Weaknesses of Most Significant
                                       Competitor:

1. _____   _____

2. _____   _____

3. _____   _____

4. _____   _____

5. _____   _____

6. _____   _____

YOUR NEW STORE: _____

Goods/Services:

Image/Positioning:

Objectives For Store Opening:

OUTLINE APPROVAL: _____ DATE:_____

TEAM NUMBER: _____
STORE NAME: _____

┌───┐
│ ***WHO WILL YOU BE COMPETING FOR BUSINESS WITH? WHO WILL YOU BE*** │
│ ***COMPETING FOR CUSTOMERS WITH?***   │
│ <u>Assignment</u>: Visit at least 2 of your proposed stores' key competitors to learn about their │
│ strengths and weaknesses. Complete the attached survey questions for as many competitors you │
│ visit Make sure to collect shopping bags, credit card applications, copies of advertisements, etc. │
└───┘

Competitor Number: _____
Competitor Name: _____
Competitor Location: _____

I. SURVEY

1.   List the mix of goods and services offered.

2.   What is its pricing orientation?

3.   Identify the promotional methods of the store (sales, etc.).

4.   Describe the way the store communicates with the customer—image, visuals, salespeople, appearance, and the "total retailing experience" of the store. (Bring in examples.)

5.   What is the store's image or positioning (for example, Bloomingdale's is trendy and upscale)?

II. POSITIONING GRID

Now, complete and attach a positioning grid for your competitive set, following the example of Figure 3-7 in the text, using two dimensions important to the potential customer of your new store.

TEAM ASSIGNMENT #3: Customer Lifestyle Profile Analysis
Due Date: _____

TEAM NUMBER: _____
STORE NAME: _____

Your new retail store should be designed to meet the needs and desires of your consumer, your shopper. Without a loyal following of customers or a lot of impulse shoppers, your store will be empty!!

<u>WHO WILL YOU BE ATTRACTING TO YOUR STORE? WHO DO YOU WANT TO SHOP THERE? WHY WILL THEY SHOP THERE? WHAT IS THEIR DECISION-MAKING PROCESS?</u>

Assignment: Go to the competitive stores you evaluated from assignment #2. You are a consumer market researcher. Through observation and interviewing at least 3 customers, develop a consumer profile consisting of the following three elements:

PART I: DEMOGRAPHICS
- What is your age?
- Are you married/single?
- Do you have children?
- Where do you live?
- Where do you work?
- What do you do for work?
- What do you do for leisure activities?

PART II: SHOPPING ATTITUDES AND BEHAVIOR
- What do you think of this store (service, products, etc.)?
- How did you choose this store to shop in?
- What is another store you would have considered for the same or similar purchase?
- How far would you travel for this type of purchase?
- What is the biggest single risk in making this purchase?

PART III: DECISION-MAKING PROCESS
- In an average week, how much time do you spend shopping (including Internet shopping)?
- Do you shop alone or with friends?
- How do you choose the stores you frequent?
- How do you choose the items you purchase?
- Did you purchase anything today?
- What were some of the other purchases you were considering <u>instead of</u> the one you purchased?
- What were some of the other purchases you were considering <u>in addition to</u> the one you purchased?

- What was the one most important thing that influenced your decision to purchase this item?
- How important was price to your decision?
- How important was the brand to your decision?

TEAM ASSIGNMENT #4: Location/Layout
Due Date: _____

TEAM NUMBER: _____
STORE NAME: _____

Choosing Your Retail Store Location
(This is a two-step exercise.)

I.   ANALYZE YOUR TRADING AREA

1.   Provide three key facts of secondary data on your <u>primary trading area's</u> population (use census data).

2.   Describe your <u>secondary trading area,</u> which contains an additional 15 to 25 percent of your store's customers.

3.   Now, referring to Figure 9-5, attach a diagram of your store's location as situated to the competitive stores within the:
   - primary trading area.
   - secondary trading area.
   - fringe trading area.

Clearly label the competitive stores.

II.   CHOOSE YOUR LOCATION

You are opening a new store in a regional shopping center. Here are the guidelines:
- You are replacing any store at the mall and you can choose more than one store to "take over the space."
- You are assuming similar traffic as the existing store you have taken over.
- You cannot change any of the entrances, exits, or services at the mall.

Outline, using the following evaluation criteria, why your team chose your retail store location:
- Pedestrian Traffic
- Vehicular Traffic
- Parking Facilities
- Store Composition—retail balance
- Specific Site Chosen—size, visibility

Competitors: Summarize the key competitors (i.e., next door neighbors) in terms of threats and opportunities to your store—good location, brand, large space, etc. Indicate which are destination competitors and parasite competitors.

TEAM ASSIGNMENT #5: Pricing/Financial Goals
Due Date: _____

TEAM NUMBER: _____
STORE NAME: _____

Retail Store Opening: Strategy Assumptions

A retail strategy is the overall plan or framework of action that guides a retail operation.

ASSIGNMENT: Based on assignments 1 to 4, make some key assumptions about your new retail business and then use these assumptions to determine the retail sales for your store.

Assumption 1: Estimate the customer traffic flow in the store on an annual basis using the following formula:

i.   (Number of days per week open X 52 weeks) X number of hours open each day = Number of total hours open per year _____

ii.   (Number of customers visiting your store per hour - on average) = _____

iii.   i. X ii. = total number of customers visiting your store each year, or traffic flow: _____

Assumption 2: "Guesstimate" the annual retail purchases using the following formula and the number in iii above:

iv.   % of those visiting the store actually purchasing something = _____%

v.   Range of 3 price points for your store merchandise selection = low, average, and high

vi.   Adding up to 100%, how do your purchases break down by these 3 price points:
   * Low: ___ % of purchases
   * Average: ___ % of purchases
   * High: _____ % of purchases

vii.   Combine:
   * (Number of customers visiting store) X (each % in vi. for low, average, high) = # of purchases made by each price point = _____ low, _____ average, _____ high
   * Add together (# of customers in above) X (each of the corresponding price points) = total retail sales of store in year 1

Assumption 3: Use actual profit and loss statement % contribution as a guideline to develop your budget and profit plan:

Net sales = (from vii.)   _____

Cost of goods sold (45% of net sales)   _____

Gross profit = Net sales – Cost of goods sold   _____

Operating expenses: _____

Advertising: _____

Operational (other):   _____

      Total operating expenses: _____

Net profit = Gross profit - Total operating expenses   _____

TEAM NUMBER: _____
STORE NAME: _____

STEP 1. **Define Your Merchandising Philosophy**
- Sets the guidelines for all merchandise decisions.
- Drives every product decision, including display, visuals, pricing.
- Reflects the store's marketplace positioning and is designed to appeal to the store's primary customer.

STEP 2. **Devise Your Merchandise Plan (include assumptions on merchandise assortment and collect pictures of representative merchandise)**
- Assortment (assortment is the selection of merchandise carried in the store). Is the assortment wide (the number of distinct goods) or deep (variety within one class of goods)?
- Merchandise Mix—What are the types of merchandise to be sold? Classify the merchandise in the assortment by basic, seasonal, and, fad) and by level of innovativeness (new goods, trends, or "safer" basics).
- Allocate the percent of branded and private branded merchandise, and within each:
  1. By price point (use data from assignment #5).
  2. By basic, seasonal, trend.

STEP 3. **Calculate Your Inventory Spending Budget by Price Point and by Type of Merchandise**

Price Points	Basic	Seasonal	Trend	Total Purchases
Low =				
Average =				
High =				
Total Retail $ Inventory				***

***Use answer from vii. X 120% to account for inventory levels.

TEAM NUMBER: _____
STORE NAME: _____

This is a challenging assignment. There are 3 equally important parts:

    I.   **Your store's shopping bag**
    II.   **Your store's image**
    III.   **Your store's promotional efforts including advertisement your store's launch event**

I. SHOPPING BAG

- Students will use a shopping bag as a format for identifying the target shopper for their new retail store.
- The shopping bag will represent the image and lifestyle of the store and be consistent with the advertising message planned for the store.

MATERIALS

- One paper shopping bag with handle for each team's new store opening; resource materials on target shopping habits including competitive advertising, retailer Internet site images, and fashion statements.
- Required backup for assignment to include samples of competitive shopping bags, statement of store mission, and customer profile (1 page).

WRITTEN FORMAT

- The written presentation should include:
  1. Design objectives.
  2. Store mission.
  3. Customer profile.
  4. Competitive environment/shopping bags.
  5. Summary of key purpose of your shopping bag.

II. STORE IMAGE

1. Establish your communication strategy—how you will attract the customer
2. Define your store atmosphere—physical characteristics/general interior
   - Sign
   - Lighting
   - Flooring
   - Colors
   - Aisles
3. Design your traffic flow patterns—functional product groupings
4. Create your window

III. "LAUNCH YOUR STORE CONCEPT"
1.   Take your advertising budget and determine how you want to spend it. Remember that you must keep within that budget for the entire year.

YOU MUST HAVE REAL, CREATED EXAMPLES OF ALL OF YOUR ADVERTISING AND PROMOTIONAL EFFORTS!!!

Refer to the following chart for costs of advertising and promotional activities. Fill in your store's budget and rationale for each item.

TEAM ASSIGNMENT #7: Store Image/Promotion/Shopping Bag *(continued)*
Date Due: _____

ADVERTISING AND PROMOTIONAL BUDGET FOR
TEAM NUMBER: _____
STORE NAME: _____

BUDGET ITEM	AVERAGE COSTS/DETAILS	YOUR STORE BUDGET	RATIONALE
TV commercial	Production: $150,000-$300,000 Placement: $25,000-$50,000/minute cable $500,000-$1,000,000/minute prime time		
Print ad in magazine	Ad Creation: $50,000-$75,000 per ad Placement: $50,000-$85,000 per one page in one magazine per month		
Print ad in newspaper	Ad Creation:$15,000 per ad Placement: $25,000 per ad per day per newspaper		
Radio campaign	1 month on one radio station = $150,000		
Bus campaign	Per major city bus line per month = $150,000		
Billboards	Per billboard per city per month = $50,000-$150,000 plus $15,000 production of each billboard visual		
Couponing	Usually face value of coupon plus $12.50 per thousand for mailing and handling		
Launch party	$50-$250 per person for cocktails $150,000 guest appearance $20,000 giveaways		

YOUR STORE'S ASSUMPTIONS FOR BUDGET SELECTIONS:

1.

2.

3.

4.